IN HARNESS AT HISTON

GU00504508

Cover photograph courtesy of The Cambridgeshire Collection

Also available from Horsley Press:

Boy on a Branch
A King's Lynn and Isle of Ely Boyhood
by Cyril Marsters

Cyril Marsters

IN HARNESS AT HISTON

Working on Chivers Farms in the 1940s

The Horsley Press

III

First published in Great Britain in 2009
by The Horsley Press
King's Lynn

Reprinted 2011

ISBN 978-0-9524493-2-4

Printed by
King's Lynn Press Ltd
Austin Fields, King's Lynn
Telephone: 01553 773011

The Horsley Press
Email: info@horsleypress.co.uk

CONTENTS

Part 1.

Part 2.

NOTES ON THE TEXT:

*Although recollections of the various jobs done on the farm come to mind quite clearly and have been described as accurately as possible, it is not achievable at this distance in time to put them all into **exact** sequence, though this has been done where known. All other items are an amalgam from more than one year. However, for the sake of interest, the following portrait of my employment on the Chivers farms is written as a continuous narrative..*

Author

ACKNOWLEDGEMENTS:

Proof Reading: *Many thanks to my wife Ruth and daughters Helen and Zillah for their diligence in proof reading the text.*

Pictures: *Cover photograph and all photographs within the text, with the exception of that on page 119, are courtesy of The Cambridgeshire Collection, to whom I express my appreciation.*

NB. All the pictures were actually taken on the Chivers Farms

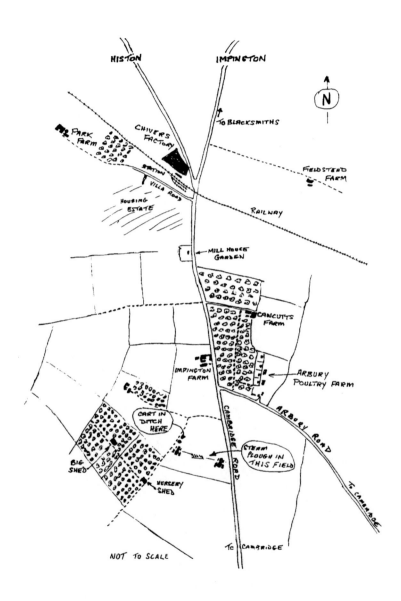

HISTON   IMPINGTON

N

TO BLACKSMITHS

PARK FARM

CHIVERS FACTORY

FIELDSTEAD FARM

STATION

VILLA ROAD

HOUSING ESTATE

RAILWAY

MILL HOUSE GARDEN

CANCUTTS FARM

IMPINGTON FARM

ARBURY POULTRY FARM

CART IN DITCH HERE

ARBURY ROAD

BIG SHED

STEAM PLOUGH IN THIS FIELD

CAMBRIDGE ROAD

TO CAMBRIDGE

NURSERY SHED

NOT TO SCALE

TO CAMBRIDGE

VII

IN HARNESS AT HISTON'
by
Cyril Marsters

Preface

On looking back on my life, it seems to split naturally into different periods. The first period covers my childhood in King's Lynn, Norfolk, from my birth on 14th May 1928 to just after the beginning of World War Two in 1939. At this time my father, Len Marsters, was a railwayman, working for the London & North Eastern Railway Company (L.N.E.R.) at the nearby station.

The second period began about mid-March in 1940 when the family moved to, what was then, the Isle of Ely, in Cambridgeshire, to the little country railway station of Wilburton, where Dad was to take charge. The station was on the L.N.E.R branch line from Ely to St. Ives and we lived in the station house. During this period I left school and started work myself, as a signal-box boy at Ely North Junction. Whilst we were at Wilburton Dad contracted tuberculosis in his spine and had to leave us for a long spell in hospital. On 24 November 1943 the hospital fitted Dad with a back-support and something that had been half expected, now became very clear: that when he eventually left hospital he would be unable to resume his job at the station. This being the case, the L. N. E. R. said that when Dad was ready for work again, they would provide him with a light job at Cambridge station. Therefore, about the end of November 1943 the family moved from Wilburton to live in Cambridge.

My boyhood adventures during the above *'King's Lynn'* and *'Wilburton'* periods are recounted in my book 'Boy on a Branch'. Now, towards the end of 1943 when we arrived in Cambridge, a third period of new experiences was about to begin. Circumstances were now to allow me to do something I had really wanted to do when I had left school – to work on a farm – and the following is a description of my experiences on Chivers' Farms at Histon from January 1944 to June 1948.

1

At this time tractors were increasingly being used in agriculture, to replace horses, so I count myself fortunate that I was able to experience working with the famous Chivers' Percheron horses. The Chivers' stables of these fine animals were still providing the motive power for the greater proportion of the cultivation and haulage on their farms during this period. This book, then, which I have called 'In Harness at Histon', is a sequel to 'Boy on a Branch'. My hope is that those people who have told me how much they enjoyed the earlier book, will be equally entertained by this new one.

****

Cambridge

The house in Cambridge into which we moved was No. 56 Eden Street. It was an old, neglected house that had been located by some young Cambridge friends who had kindly cleaned up the house before we moved in. They had made enquiries about the property but, strangely, no-one knew who the owner was and the house appeared to have been abandoned. We quickly settled in and got everything shipshape, but it was a great disappointment that Dad's discharge from hospital was not going to take place in time for him to be home with us for Christmas.

Before we had left Wilburton, as well as offering to provide Dad with a job at Cambridge, the Railway Company had promised to transfer me to a box-boy's job in a Cambridge signal-box. On the first Monday morning after our arrival at Eden Street, I therefore presented myself at Cambridge station and was taken to one of the boxes and introduced to the signal-man in charge and his box-boy. I think the box was the one located just below the Mill Road bridge. My first disappointment was to find that, instead of the 'man-sized' levers of the Ely North Junction box, this one had silly looking tiny handles that were operated with no effort whatsoever, with the fingers! Instead of a manual box, this one was an 'electric' one

Strictly speaking, the box-boy is not employed to work the levers – which is the signal-man's job – his duties are mainly to keep the records of the signalling operations. However, it is usually the practice for the box-boy to have a go on the 'frame' and I knew that I was going to miss the manual box I had been used to. Having been promised, as I had thought, a transfer to this box, I had assumed that the current boy was leaving the box for another job. I spent two weeks in learning the slightly different aspects of the Cambridge box but then, at the end of the fortnight it became clear that there was no vacancy for me, and I was asked to report for duty, next week, to help out in the goods-yard office.

On arrival home I complained bitterly about the situation to Mum and said I thought I would leave the L N E R. I reminded her that when I had left school, I had expressed the wish to work on a farm, but she had dissuaded me from doing so and steered me towards the railway. Although I had thoroughly enjoyed my time working in the Ely box, at Cambridge the glamour of the job had gone and I now determined that I would try for the kind of work I had initially been drawn to. Much to my surprise, this time Mum made no objection and agreed that we would look out for a suitable job.

Mum lost no time in the matter of my job seeking and enlisted the help of one of the members of our local Church, a Mr Albert Vyse. Mr Vyse was apparently in touch with country matters and the farming community. He had a number of business interests but his main one at the time, I believe, was work he did for the Milk Marketing Board. This involved him in visits to, and contacts with, numerous farms and farmers – hence Mum's decision to ask for his assistance. He promised he would do his best to help and said he would contact us again as soon as possible.

The Christmas period then intervened, but Mr Vyse was as good as his word, and soon after Christmas he told us that he had contacted the Manager of Chivers Farms, whom he knew, and had told him about my desire to work on a farm. The Manager had agreed to see me for an interview, in his office, located at the premises of the Chivers factory at Histon. Mr Vyse said that he would pick me up in his car to take me to Histon for the interview; this would have been in the New Year (1944). It was fairly obvious that Mr Vyse had paved the way with the Manager for me to be given a job, for he also instructed that I could attend in suitable *working* clothes, because it had been agreed that, subject to the interview going OK, I could start work immediately.

On the Monday morning I put on my heavy gardening boots, and other clothes I thought suitable and was picked up by Mr Vyse, as arranged, for the drive to Histon. I cannot recall the Farm Manager's name, but he was a very pleasant man and put me at my ease. The interview was quite short, during which he asked such questions as to my reasons for wishing to take up farm work; how I would get to work, etc. He told me that Mr Vyse, who knew my family, had vouched for me as being of good character and, as he himself was satisfied with the interview, he was happy to give me a job and, if I wished I could start straightway. After the interview Mr Vyse, who had been waiting in the outer office, arranged that he would pick me up after the day's work to take me home again; the place and time for this having been arranged, he then left.

First day at Chivers: Park Farm

The Manager led me out of the office to his car outside, to take me to where I was to work. Leaving the factory we crossed over the railway crossing and then turned right into a road which, the Manager explained, led to one of the Chivers' farms – named Park Farm. However, we did not reach the farm-yard itself. On the right-hand side of the roadway we came to an orchard of large apple trees and I suddenly spotted ahead a pair of plough handles sticking out of the trees towards the roadway. As we approached I saw an elderly man sitting on a rolled up piece of sacking on the plough. He stood up as we got out of the car and the manager introduced us to each other. The ploughman was Mr Sid Parker, the Park Farm head horse-keeper. His two horses, hitched to the front of the plough in tandem formation, were standing quietly nearby within the trees.

Having made the introductions, the farms manager left me with Sid and returned to his office. I was told that the boy who had been leading the trace-horse for him had had to go home, sick, and I was now there to replace him. Never having handled a horse before, this prospect was at once both exciting and rather daunting. Sid took me to the front of the horses and showed me how to hold the 'leader' – a long cord which hung down to the ground from the near-side of the trace-horse's bit. I was to hold it with my right hand about nine inches below the horse's chin and to take up the slack end in my left hand. "Now, boy" he said, "lead him straight down the row. When you get to the end go right across the headland, then pull him round towards you – we're coming back down the next row but one".

We started off down the row and I was surprised how little the horse seemed to need 'leading'. He progressed along the row smoothly and quite straight without any guidance from me as I loosely held his leader. When we reached the end of the row, things were different! Now, whether Sid thought I'd had previous experience, or whether he decided to teach me my first real lesson, I don't know. I carried on straight across the headland as instructed before pulling the horse towards me to start the turn. In my ignorance, I stayed too close to the horse, without realising the trajectory taken by a horse's front feet when he is required to turn sharply. A massive hoof was lifted and swiftly plonked down sideways towards me, landing on the toe of my boot, pushing it down into the soft ground. Stuck in the mud I panicked, sure that I was going to be knocked down and trampled on. A more experienced reaction –which I didn't possess – would have been to yell 'Whoa' and stop the horses. Instead I managed to yank my foot out and move fast away from the horse.

How much of my scare had been seen by Sid, I'm not sure. He never said anything about it. Much of the time afterwards we seemed to turn mainly to the right at the end of the rows, but when we did have to turn left, having learned my lesson, I was ready to avoid horse's hooves. Working with the horses was a completely new experience but, gradually getting to know what to expect of them, I felt that I was going to enjoy horse-work. About 1 o' clock Sid decided that it was time to stop for some 'dockey'. I sat on the ground on a folded sack given me by Sid and opened the sandwiches that Mum had packed for me. Sid also sat on a folded sack, but instead of on the ground, he sat rather more comfortably on the frame of his plough.

5

As we ate I was able to observe Sid more closely than I been able to up until then. I would guess that he was approaching sixty years of age. He was quite sprightly, which of course he needed to be in order to manhandle his plough each time he turned at the row ends. He wore corduroy breeches, heavy leather boots and shaped, stiff, leather gaiters round his lower legs. On his upper parts he wore a thick shirt, a heavy jacket and a broad-brimmed hat. To me he looked the quintessential ploughman. He seemed a rather mild mannered man, easy to get on with, and as the next few days went by it was to be a pleasure working with him.

About 3 o'clock we stopped ploughing. It was time Sid said, to take the horses back up to the farm. He showed me how the horses were unyoked from the plough and how to hang up the trace chains clear of their legs. He also showed me the easiest way of carrying my haversack – in which I had brought my dockey tin, thermos flask and my mackintosh. This was hung on the near-side hame of the trace-horse's collar. It was the standard practice, I later found, to use the collar hame as a useful support for carrying all sorts of items. We walked the horses, one each, along the roadway the short distance from the orchard to the farm.

On arrival at the farmyard Sid led the way into the stables with his horse. I followed him in with the trace-horse, under instruction from Sid to keep the horse in the middle of the doorway as we went through, to avoid catching the harness on the door-posts. Inside, the stable was divided into four bays, each wide enough for one horse with room at each side to walk round it. Each bay had a manger on the rear wall, with a metal hayrack above it in the corner. The bays were divided by wooden partitions that sloped up towards the rear wall to prevent the horses reaching their neighbour's hay. About fifteen minutes after our arrival another man arrived back, bringing two more horses. He was the farm under-horseman, about forty years of age, thickset and very

Ploughing team working abreast.
(Photograph courtesy of The Cambridgeshire Collection)

powerfully built. If my memory serves me correctly, I think his name was Walter Coxall [1] Walter had returned to the stable with his team, on his own I noticed – he had no boy with him. The reason for this, I learned, was that he had been ploughing in an arable field with his

---

[1] *Slight doubt here as to whether I have given the name of an Impington Farm horseman instead of the Park Farm one (see same name mentioned in my Diary Entry for 18 November 1947).*

horse team working abreast, and had not needed a boy. In the orchards there was not enough room to use a team abreast – there it was necessary to work the horses in tandem, hence the use of a boy to lead the trace horse.

Although the main work of the day was over, I soon learned that there was plenty of work yet to be done in the stables. The harness had to be removed from the horses and they had to be fed and groomed. Sid showed me how to take off the harness of my trace horse and to carefully hang it up on the special supports on the wall to the rear of the horses. Meanwhile, a bit further along Walter was doing the same for his team. I had just been shown by Sid how to take off my horse's collar – it had to be twisted upside down round the narrow part of the neck before you could get it over the horses head – when we heard a car drive into the yard outside. Shortly after, Mr Vyse appeared in the stable doorway; he had come to pick me up after my first day's work, as arranged. We had by no means finished the stable jobs, but Sid suggested that I call it a day and go home, and he would expect to see me at 7 am next morning.

During the drive home to Eden Street Mr Vyse asked how my day had gone. I was enthusiastic about the horses; I told him I was sure that I would enjoy the work at Chivers and thanked him for all he had done in obtaining the job for me. That evening I checked over my bicycle to make sure that it was OK for the ride to work the following morning, when I would have to cycle to Histon. On the front of the bike, attached to the handlebars, I had a large cycle-basket which had been made by Italian prisoners of war and which I had acquired when they had been at Wilburton filling in the parachute mine crater. This basket was now going to be very useful in carrying my dockey bag and mackintosh etc. to work.

Park Farm continued.
I was up bright and early next morning, cycled to Histon and arrived at Park Farm just before 7 am. Sid and Walter were both in the stable and the horses were finishing their first feed of the day. Next job was to harness up and Sid showed me how to harness my horse. This was

done in the reverse order to which the harness had been removed the previous afternoon. Firstly the collar was put on and I was surprised when I lifted the collar, bottom side up, at how co-operative the horse was in allowing me to push it over his head. It was then a case of reaching up and twisting the collar round, at the narrow part of the neck, to the right way up and finally, taking the weight of the collar with a hand underneath and allowing it to fall back into place on the horse's shoulders. The trace harness seemed more complicated but, with Sid's guidance it was eventually fitted to his satisfaction, with the chains neatly hooked up clear of the horse's legs. It didn't take Sid long to harness the other horse and we were ready for the day's work.

Leaving the farm we started up the road towards the orchard; Walter meanwhile had already left with his team to wherever it was he was working. On getting back to where the plough was, Sid attached his plough horse to the front of the plough and then got me to hook the trace horse up at the front. Before we started ploughing again, Sid removed his dockey bag, coat etc. from where he had hung them on the horse's hame, and I did the same with mine. These were placed in a safe place close to one of the tree trunks for use later at dockey time. The day went well; the weather was fine and I enjoyed the freedom of working with the horses in the open air. Sid had told me on the previous day of the times of the meal breaks on the farm, and after two hours of walking with the horses I had quite an appetite for the first break of the day, 'breakfast' at 9 am., for which half an hour was allowed.

During 'dockey' the previous day I had observed Sid's unusual way of eating and wondered whether this would be repeated today. It was repeated and I assumed that it was his regular method. Our two breakfasts were similar in that they were both made up of bread and cheese – but in a slightly different form. Mine were sandwiches; Sid's was a large chunk off the end of a loaf, about 2 inches or more thick, with a single lump of cheese. Taking a shut-knife from his jacket pocket, Sid cut a sliver of crust from the side of the loaf, placed the cheese on the bread and the piece of crust on top of the cheese. Then, holding the whole arrangement in his left hand, with his thumb firmly clamped on top of the crust, proceeded to carefully cut off alternate slivers of bread and cheese to place in his mouth. I am afraid that I had gobbled my sandwiches down in half the time it took Sid to finish his breakfast. When, as young children, we had hurried the eating of our food Mum had told us that "each mouthful should be chewed thirty times". I thought of this and wondered what she would have thought of Sid's method of dealing with his bread and cheese; she certainly could not object, I thought, to his leisurely way of eating.

When our half-hour break was up, we started ploughing again, continuing until 'dockey' break at about 1 o'clock. We had just finished the break when we received a visit from a man on a bike who, I would guess, to be in his forties. After chatting to Sid about the ploughing, he asked me how I was getting on. His name was Harry Chambers who, I learned, was the farms foreman. Up to this point, having become acquainted only with Sid and Walter at Park Farm, I had no idea of the extent of the Chivers Farms organisation. There were a number of other farms around Histon, of which Mr Chambers was foreman, in charge of their day to day running. The ones I was to become familiar with, in addition to Park Farm, were: Impington Farm, Cawcutts Farm, and the Poultry Farm.

After the foreman left us, pedalling off on his bike, we started ploughing again. The afternoon went quite well and I was getting more familiar with handling the horse. Every now and again, after we had turned in at the end of a row of trees, Sid would stop for a few minutes to give the horses a breather. This was also an opportunity for us to have a drink. In addition to my Thermos flask – which held enough hot drink for the two meal breaks - I had brought a bottle of fruit squash in my dockey bag for the between break stops. Sid would drink from his bottle of cold tea.

When we got back to the farm after the afternoon's ploughing, I was able to take a share in the routine in the stables this time, without interruption for, having my bike at the farm, I was not reliant on Mr Vyse to take me home. Sid showed me once more how to un-harness the horse. Then he led me through a door at the end of the stables into an adjoining building where there was a heap of mangolds and a root grinder. This metal machine which stood on four splayed legs, had a large hopper and a handle on the front, which was turned by hand, for grinding up the roots. Sid took a two-tined fork which had been standing in a corner and showed me how spear some of the mangolds with the tines of the fork and drop them into the hopper. Explaining that some ground mangolds were needed for part of the horses' 'baits', he left me to grind them up. As I turned the handle, the ground-up product of my efforts fell into a metal container placed below the machine.

While I was occupied with the grinder, Walter was busy mixing chaff and crushed oats. Every few minutes he would come to me and, using a hand scoop, would take a generous portion of the juicy ground-up mangolds from under the grinder and combine them with his oats and chaff. This gave the whole mixture a nice moist consistency. Each horse's ration was carried in a special kind of sieve and tipped into the manger in front of the horse. The round sieve was about 2 feet in diameter, the sides of about 4 inches high were made of some kind of wood, bent round in a circle and the bottom was composed of split cane. When all four horses had their own rations and were busy eating, the next job – on which Sid had already started – was to groom them. I was shown how to do this, firstly using a curry-comb to remove the loose hair and dust, then using a brush to give a final shine. You started the grooming at the top of the horse's neck and worked downwards, including down its legs, then along its back and sides towards its rear end. Meanwhile as you worked a contented munching sound came from each of the four horses.

When the grooming had been completed, Walter, starting at one end of the stable commenced an inspection of the horses' feet. Picking up the right front leg of the first horse, he cleaned out the dirt and mud from under the hoof, using a special knife. He then systematically worked his way clockwise round the horse doing the same with each foot. After doing three of the horses he asked me to have a go at the fourth one; the trace-horse I had been leading during the day. I found that picking up the horse's front leg was fairly simple as, with the leg bent it could be held comfortably with the left hand under the hoof, whilst cleaning out with the right hand. Back legs were not so easy. Here, to get at the underneath of the hoof the leg had to be slightly pulled backwards and held between ones knees, and I found this rather an awkward thing to do. However, I managed the job to Walter's satisfaction and was pleased that I had learned one more lesson in looking after a heavy horse. I was surprised at just how co-operative all the horses were during this task, just munching away at their feed, quite unconcerned.

I was now getting used to the horses and was enjoying working with Sid, who was a very pleasant little man. However, although I was not aware of it, my time at Park Farm was not to last much longer. The following day we received another visit from Harry Chambers, the farm foreman. Seeing that the ploughing was progressing well across the orchard, he asked Sid how long he thought it would take to finish. Sid said that he thought that one more day after this would about see the job done. Harry, turning to me, told me that after we had finished work here, in future I was to report for work each morning to Impington Farm – located on the Cambridge road.

The next two days passed quite swiftly, with the ploughing, followed by the afternoon routine in the stable. On the second day we finished in the orchard about thirty minutes earlier than we normally left off, and so we were back at the farm a little early. To occupy my time once the routine jobs were done, Sid got me onto cleaning some of the harness until leaving off time. I was sorry that my short time at Park Farm had come to an end, and wondered what to expect the following day at the other farm. I had not yet visited Impington Farm, but I knew where it was as I passed its entrance on the Cambridge road each day as I had cycled to Park Farm.

Impington Farm
I arrived at the gates of Impington Farm about five minutes to seven the next morning. There were already a number of men waiting outside the gate, with others still arriving, including a number of boys. At seven o'clock the gates were opened and Mr Chambers came out. Taking each man or boy in turn he told him about the job he was to do that day,

following which each one would disappear, either through the gate into the farm-yard, or off on their bikes to various other locations. This, I learned was the regular routine each morning. Some men, when they were on a job that would take some time to carry out, would have been instructed to go straight to the work site each morning without reporting at the farm. Those having finished a job would have to report to find out what they were to do next.

When it came to my turn Harry told me he wanted me to lead horses for a man named George. Telling me to put my bike away round the back of the farmyard, then to go to the stable, he said he would see me there in a few minutes. When I found the stable building I was surprised at the difference between it and the one I had got used to at Park Farm. Through the doorway, in the middle of the long front wall, and just across a wide gangway along the inside of the wall, stretched a row of at least ten, maybe a dozen, horses with their rear ends towards me. Their noses were all directed at the far-side wall, along which was a continuous wooden manger with hayrack above. Each horse stood with space enough between to be able to get round them, but there were no divisions between, such as the ones at Park Farm. This stable was completely 'open-plan' as it were.

There were a number of men busy harnessing up the horses, whilst the horses themselves were finishing off the last of their morning feed. Each horse had a hemp halter and was tethered through a ring on the manger, which restricted its sideways reach somewhat – though I noticed that some of them tried to steal their immediate neighbours' feed. The stable was a bustle of activity, with a rattle of chains as the harness was put on and one by one the men left with either one, or a team of horses. By the time Harry appeared in the stable most of the men and horses had left for work. Only two horses remained in the stable, a horse right at the end, next to the left–hand end wall, and next to him a mare – both white. The horse was relatively small one, probably the smallest I had seen in the stable, and putting the finishing touches to their harnessing was a short, elderly-looking man who I assumed to be 'George'. Harry introduced us, told George that I would be leading for him, and then left without further ado. I think that

George must have been at least sixty years of age; he was a short, wizened little man and the reception I got from him was not very encouraging. He was very brusque and as different from Sid as chalk and cheese. "Know how to lead a horse?" he snapped? "Yes" I replied.

"Right" barked George, "Take the mare out into the yard – and don't catch the door-posts". I undid the halter, backed the mare away from the manger and started to turn her round to leave the stable, holding the 'lead' a little below the mare's chin as I had been taught by Sid. There was another shout from George: "That's not the way to hold a horse – you can't control her like that" he growled, "Here, let me show you". Taking the lead out of my hand, he took up all the slack in his left hand and, dispensing with the use of the lead, grabbed the ring on the end of the horse's 'bit', together with the end of the leather bridle rein, close alongside the horse's mouth. "There" he said, as he swung the mare's head from side to side, "You can control her like this!"

Not at all happy with George's manner, I nevertheless held the mare close to her bit as he had instructed, and led her outside into the yard. Holding a horse in this manner turned out to be useful on occasions, but it was not as comfortable or free and easy as holding her lead a little lower down – nor was it necessary all the time. However, George's word was law and, as long as I was with him, I had to hold the ring at the end of the bit. Another thing he insisted on when I was leading for him, was that my arm was to be held out straight. This again, so he said, was in the interest of controlling the horse. It was rather, I think, in the interest of George controlling his boy! Boys seemed to be regarded by George as a necessary evil – you had to put up with them, but they needed to be strictly controlled and kept in their place. All this I was to find out the hard way a little later.

When George himself emerged from the stable with the little horse, before we moved off to go to where the ploughing was to be done he indulged in a little habit that I was to witness daily all the time I was to work with him. In the range of buildings outside the stable was a loft, and leading up to the loft door, stood a set of solid wooden steps.

George manoeuvred his horse alongside the ladder, climbed up a few steps and then, holding the near-side collar hame, clumsilly lowered himself backwards onto the horse's back. When he had made himself comfortable we set off for the work site, with George riding 'side-saddle' and me walking behind him with the mare. The orchard we were to plough was some distance from the farm 'down the fen' and the first part of the distance was along a stretch of the public road. Whilst on the road, we kept in single file, and on the right-hand side facing oncoming traffic.

Leading for 'Old George'
We turned right onto a farm roadway, and after passing a number of arable fields we eventually arrived at an area that was predominantly orchard. The area we were to start on was a fairly new plantation of young pear trees. These were all in neat rows and were interspersed, in the rows, with gooseberry bushes – three bushes to each space between the trees. The rows of trees and bushes had been liberally covered with an application of farm-yard manure, in a band of about four feet wide along the rows. It was the wider strips between the tree rows that we were to plough, turning the soil over towards the manure. In the corner of the plantation, next to the farm roadway was a large wooden shed, which I later came to know as the 'Nursery' shed. Before we started ploughing, George decided that we would hang up our dockey bags and our coats in the shed. George's plough stood a short distance away from the shed and later I learned that it had been delivered there ready for us, on one of the four-wheeled pony lorries, which were used on the farm for all sorts of delivery jobs.

The next job, of course, was to yoke the horses to the plough and I prepared myself to assist George with this, as I had been used to doing at Park Farm for Sid. George, however had other ideas and insisted on doing everything himself. After yoking his horse to the plough, and then my mare on the front, he gave me another demonstration of how I was to hold the mare. "Take hold of her bearing rein like this" he barked, as he grabbed the leather rein close to her mouth, with half the metal ring at the end of the bit inside his palm as well. I took hold of the rein just behind the ring, but that wasn't good enough and George

15

insisted that I hold it right up against her mouth by holding the ring as well.

When George had arranged all this to his satisfaction, he walked out a little way along the roadway with the ends of the tree rows on his left, to decide which two rows he wanted us to turn into. Having decided on the chosen entry point he ordered that we move along the headland towards it. When his plough was at the right position he called 'whoa' and we stopped. The trace horse and I now being slightly ahead of this point, would obviously have to turn to the left and come back slightly in a kind of semi-circle, in order to gain entry between the trees. This thought now made me apprehensive, bearing in mind the incident when I had first turned Sid's horses towards me and had my foot trodden into the mud. And this time, I was not to have that bit of space which the holding of the leader would have given me – no, I had to pull the mare towards me whilst holding her close to her bit.

When I started the sharp left turn into the trees, having to hold the mare so closely, there was no need to remind me of George's second requirement, that I was to keep my arm straight when leading. I did it automatically, in order to keep the maximum space between me and those front hooves which were splaying down towards me. In my inexperience, that turn seemed absolutely awkward and clumsy, and I was relieved when we were finally in position within the trees. George positioned his plough and then, using the heavy-looking plough spanner, which had hung from its special slot on the plough frame, he adjusted the plough for the work in hand. Having moved the wheels to suitable height, and the hake at the front to get the desired position for the line of draft, George ordered us to start. We were off, alongside the row of trees on our right and ploughing towards the strip of farmyard manure.

Although I had done this job of leading for Sid for four days at Park Farm, today was somehow different. It was not as free and easy. George appeared to be an 'old misery' and was going to be difficult to get on with; I felt a tension between us. We progressed down the row and I was quite pleased that we were to turn *right* at the end before coming round between another two rows of trees. It was to be *right turns* for most of the time, for which I was thankful. It was rather irksome having to adhere to George's instruction that when leading the horse, my arm had to be kept out straight. Whether this was on the principle that if I walked in a straight line, holding the mare close to her bit, then she could do no other than walk straight, I don't know.

The weather was dry and not too cold – quite pleasant in fact – and I was soon more relaxed and once more feeling the freedom of the open air. At first, having to keep my arm straight was rather vexing. As we moved a long, however, I learned to achieve a slight relaxation and flexibility in my arm, which George back at the plough could not detect. If you did the slightest thing that George considered not quite right, he would shout at you; he was not one to express any praise when things went well. However, I learned to live with his irritable ways and, in fact, I felt rather sorry for him. He was a very thin and wizened little man and he never seemed very well. I think that I instinctively had an inkling that his innate grumpiness and crotchety ways were heightened by his sorry physical condition and were difficult for him to control. Anyway, I worked with George for the whole of January and February of 1944 and was able to take the bad temper and disapproving comments he would throw at me during that time.

George's dress was very similar to that worn by Sid: corduroy breeches, heavy leather boots and the stiff, shaped, leather gaiters that fitted snugly over the tops of the boots. His upper attire was also like Sid's: thick shirt and a heavy jacket. To me, both Sid and George looked the typical country ploughmen. For very cold or wet weather, George had a heavy black overcoat which he wore with a piece of cord tied round the waist. I imagine that this coat had done duty as a best Sunday coat for a good number of years before being taken to use at work. Other men on the farm who wore similar breeches were Claud Archer, the foreman Harry Chambers, and Charlie Wrycroft. Claud and Harry also had leather leggings, but Charlie had thick long woollen stockings instead, and Wellington boots. Many of the general workers wore bib-and-brace overalls, and their other attire was very mixed.

Our ploughing in the pears went on quite uneventfully up until breakfast time and I was pleased that I had managed to stay on the right side of George. After we had done a few rounds, on looking at the neat rows of ploughed ridges alongside the strips of manure that had been applied along the tree rows, it occurred to me that the trees and fruit bushes looked as though they were being 'tucked up' for the winter. At nine o'clock George gathered up his plough-lines and hooked them onto the collar hames. Instead of staying where we were for breakfast, George had decided that we would have it in the 'nursery shed' where we had left our dockey bags. He un-yoked the horses, then walked the short distance to the shed with his horse, with me following on behind with the mare.

The horses were left opposite the shed, within view of the doorway, with their 'leaders' hanging down to the ground, and I followed George into the shed. I was surprised to find two other men already in the shed. One of them was lighting a fire in a small metal barrel that stood on some bricks in the middle of the shed floor. Arranged round the fire were a number of fruit boxes, metal drums, etc. obviously used for seats. George took down his dockey bag from where he had hung it and he and one of the other men settled themselves on a seat each, and I followed their example. The fire, which at first had been a bit smoky, was now going well and the man who'd been tending it joined us on the seats.

Apart from light from the fire, the only light in the shed came from the wide doorway, but the addition of the fire made the atmosphere quite pleasant. Everyone opened their dockey bags and started eating their breakfasts. George and one of the other men ate as Sid had done, using their shut-knives to cut their lumps of bread and cheese; the other man had his in sandwiches like me. There was quite a bit of chatter during the meal, partly about work, and I gathered that the two men had been hoeing round fruit bushes in another nearby plantation. Occasionally a bit of breeze through the doorway would waft a little smoke into my eyes - I had probably picked the wrong seat – but it had been enjoyable sitting round the fire and listening to the conversations.

George and I went back to the plough; he yoked up again and we started work once more. The morning was going smoothly without any complaints from George and I thought I was doing well; until one occasion when we turned in at the end of a row. Having hauled his plough round squarely ready for starting the next bout, George stopped for a while to give the horses a breather. Now, there was a strict 'No Smoking' rule on the farm, which the foreman tried, unsuccessfully, to enforce. George smoked cigarettes and sometimes when resting the horses he would light up and have a smoke. Whenever he did this, I was not allowed to go back to have a chat with him; he insisted that I stay where I was and keep hold of the horse. Becoming restless I had looked around and shuffled about a bit, which had not gone unobserved by George. Suddenly he yelled at me: "What do you think you're doing boy – making a skating rink?" He didn't say, but I supposed he was thinking that if the foreman spotted the flattened ground where I had stood, before we got it ploughed out again, he would guess we had had a rather long stop.

As already remarked, George seemed to regard boys as a necessary evil. His horses however were a different matter; I could tell that he was very fond of them. A small example of this, I think, was the way he had padded the trace chains of the mare with sacking, wound round and round the chains. I had wondered why this had been done, as I had not seen any of the other horses' traces similarly treated. I had not known earlier that the mare was in fact 'in foal', with the foal due to be born in the spring and I could only assume that George had padded her traces to protect her sides when she was working

George was known by all the farm staff as: 'Old George' and they were all aware of his grumpy nature. I spent almost all of that winter working with him, but I must say that as the weeks went by things became easier and more relaxed between us. He seemed gradually to accept that I wanted to co-operate with him; his criticisms became fewer and in time ceased, for which I was grateful. He would never dream of offering any praise – but with none of his previous nagging, working life became near perfect.

As I led the mare, holding the bearing rein close to her mouth as I had been instructed, I was aware of every slight movement of her head as she pulled. With a slight flexing of my arm I could control her without restricting these natural movements and I grew to feel at one with her. After a week or so, I wasn't just leading a horse, but felt part of a team. Walking at her side and holding her rein there was somehow a two-way connection, extending back through the mare, the plough-horse and back to George at the rear as he held his plough lines and guided the plough handles. George's past grumps were all forgiven – we were a team, moving mountains. As the horses pulled together in unison there was a very slight quickening and slowing, quickening and slowing, with each stride forward but which in no way could hide the overall sense of the steady, unified and fluid movement of the team. Words do not do justice to the feeling – it was something you became immersed in.

I think that the physical exercise I had at Chivers has stood me in good stead ever since. Often when the weather had been wet, I would be leading the horse with my boots heavy with mud; rather like weight lifting, with the weights on your boots. I became proud of my endurance and used to enjoy the effort. I would practice some deep breathing: breathing in over the space of three or four strides; hold it for two or three more, then out over the next few. This coupled with the exercise made me quite fit. There were times when I was hungrier than I would have liked. As a growing lad I didn't take kindly to the wartime food rationing. Luckily farm workers were allowed extra cheese, over and above the normal meagre ration, which helped a bit.

Winter came to an end and we entered early springtime. Ploughing in the orchards had nearly been completed and George and I had not much more to do. On our last day, before we had quite finished the orchard we were working in, we received a visit from Harry at about 8 am, who wanted to assess how long we would be. George had already estimated that we would most probably finish by about breakfast time so I assume that is what he told Harry. Standing by the mare, I could not quite catch the conversation and so neither did I hear the instructions about our next job. As he got on his bike to leave us, Harry called to George to say that he would send 'Curly' to pick up the plough. I wanted to know where we were to go next, but knew better than to ask, and thought that George might perhaps tell me at breakfast time. However, he kept the knowledge to himself and I had to wait to find out until Curly came.

The orchard site where we were working was close by a large brick shed. This was known as the 'Big Shed'. It was used for all sorts of purposes, including the repair and painting of ladders and was also often in use at meal times for any men working nearby. The nice thing about this shed was the massive fireplace built into the wall at one end. On the occasion when an orchard had been grubbed up, the roots had been saved and put in a huge heap behind the shed as it had been found that these made excellent fires for mealtimes. A couple of scaffold boards were almost permanently in place, supported by fruit boxes, across the front of the large fireplace. This was where we headed for at breakfast time on that final morning's work 'down the fen'.

After unhitching the horses, we walked with them the short distance to the shed and left them outside, within sight of the shed windows. Although we were early – it was still about 15 minutes to 9 am – we found one man, whom I knew as Wally, in the shed. Wally had been hoeing round fruit bushes with a couple of other men and had come early to the shed to get a fire going ready for breakfast time. He had a little heap of straw in the big fireplace and was arranging pieces of tree roots carefully around and on the straw, and by the time his two mates arrived the fire was going well. Soon after, Bill Butler, who was in charge of the three full-time farm women, arrived with his colleagues, Doris., Rene and Ollie; they had been picking up and burning tree prunings. By 9 o'clock therefore, the nine of us were sitting round a cheerful blazing fire.

During the winter I had experienced quite a number of these mealtime sessions in the big shed. I was a rather shy lad and didn't join very much in the conversation myself, but it was good to sit before the bright blaze of the fire and listen to the chatter of the others. Often the talk would be about work and how it should be done; sometimes about the speakers' private lives – and usually interesting to listen to. The company around the fire varied from one day to another, depending on who was working within reasonable distance of the shed. Sometimes it would be boosted by members of the orchard spraying gang, when I would hear conversation containing things like: 'lime sulphur', or 'tar oil winter wash'. When pruning was going on nearby, we were joined by the pruning staff: Herbie Hankin, Charlie Camps and Ken Fishpool. Yes, breakfast in the Big Shed was a pleasant change from the occasions when it was eaten alone with George, out in the open.

After breakfast the others began to disperse and return to their respective places of work; George and I had to wait for the arrival of Curly with his pony and lorry to fetch the plough. There were three of these rubber tyred, four wheeled pony lorries used on the farm. They were used as 'runabouts' to transport all kinds of things wherever they were needed and it was amazing how many jobs turned up to keep them busy. Curly, a short man of about thirty years of age appeared to be permanently employed on this job, using the same pony and vehicle each day. Two similar vehicles, were usually driven by younger lads on the farm. To them, the job was a very coveted one. They regarded it as far more glamorous to dash around all over the place with the ponies, than to stay working in one place, especially having to lead plough horses.

Curly arrived eventually with his pony and we walked with him to where we had finished work with the plough. The implement was fairly heavy, but between the three of us we lifted it on to the lorry without much difficulty. Curly, who never seemed to be in a hurry, was in a talkative mood, but his efforts to make conversation with George met with little more than grunts. He gave up his attempts to chat and trotted off with the plough, saying that he would see us at the Poultry Farm. I thought that the Poultry Farm was a strange destination to be taking the plough and I wondered just what our next job was to be. Anyway, as things turned out my long winter session of leading for George in the orchards was over. Before long I would experience some different jobs.

My Last Stint with George

At the end of each day when we had finished ploughing, George would ride back to the farm on his horse. Now, before our trek to the Poultry Farm, I was once more to witness his daily mounting routine. I could have easily have given him a 'leg-up' if he had allowed it, but that would have been far too undignified for George; he would rather manage on his own or die in the attempt. Reaching up to the top of the horse's collar with his left hand, and holding the crupper with his right hand, he then would stretch up and get his left foot on the trace chain, between the hame-hook and the back-band. Pulling with his hands and pushing up with his right leg he would struggle to mount. Often there would be one or two abortive attempts before he eventually managed to propel himself up onto the horse's back. Then he would swing round to sit sideways. After recovering his breath he would spend a further minute or so in rearranging the dislodged crupper beneath him and in getting comfortable.

We set off, George in front and me following behind him leading the mare. To amuse myself as we went along, I indulged in my usual habit of becoming engrossed in watching the movements of his horse. As it strode along with its characteristic emphatic action, the hooves seemed to be *placed* down onto the road rather than simply lowered. The muscles of his shoulders and legs rippled as I watched; I was captivated by this sturdy beast with his combination of strength and beauty. It was fascinating too to watch how, as he walked, the front hoof lifted off the ground at the last moment, just before the rear one landed in almost exactly the same spot. The movements seemed so unbelievably precise that I expected to see the horse kick his front heel; but he didn't.

We arrived at the Poultry Farm after about twenty minutes and found the plough already unloaded and awaiting us at the edge of a small field at the back of the farm. Curly had obviously been given help to unload by the poultry staff. The plot we were now required to plough was only a small piece apparently, though George still kept me in the dark as to what Harry had told him about the job. I think the ground was to be prepared for producing some cabbage plants, or some such purpose.

23

Normally ploughing in an open field would be done with the horses working two abreast, but in this case as I was already with George, it was obviously not worth while changing over. This meant that it fell to my lot to lead the trace-horse *straight* across the field for George's opening furrow.

Evidently for the small area we were to plough measurements were not too critical. George left me with the horses whilst he walked the length of the far headland across the field. I thought that perhaps he would be setting up some kind of marker for me to aim at. Instead, on his return he pointed out a gatepost on the far side and told me that I was to make for that. When he was ready, he said: "Lead her across to that gatepost boy – *and try to keep straight*". Now, although I was now much more comfortable with George than I had been at the beginning of the winter, the earlier uneasiness now returned. I was to be responsible for the *straightness* of his opening furrow and, if I made a mess of it I was sure that his earlier grumpiness would return with a vengeance. I would have to endure the rough edge of his tongue.

We started off across the little field with me looking hard at the distant gatepost. With my right arm stretched out straight, in the approved manner, I aimed my footsteps just to the left of the post, calculating that the mare, being nearly a yard to my right, should be heading for the post itself. How, I wondered, was I going to keep straight all the way across? In my desperate wish to keep straight, it occurred to me to do it in stages. Lowering my sight in as straight a line as I could I fixed my eyes on a large stone about ten to fifteen yards ahead. When approaching the stone I took a similar bearing on another object directly in my path, and so on until we reached the far side. I turned right at the end and, as instructed by George, brought the horse right round to come back alongside the opening furrow. To my great relief it looked pretty straight. How much of this was due to me, and how much to the skill of George, I didn't know. But I was sure that it was good enough to avoid a telling off. George said nothing.

After continuing alongside his first shallow furrow, turning the second one the other way, George set his plough deeper. He then ploughed underneath the two *'scratch'* furrows to form a ridge. I think that it was a simple matter then of ploughing round each side of this ridge until the area needed was big enough, for I do not remember having to open another furrow. After we had completed a few rounds, we had a visit from Harry. After turning the plough in at one end, George stopped to talk to him. Staying put at the head of the mare, I couldn't catch what they were saying, but I wondered what Harry thought of our work.

Before leaving us, Harry came to the front of the team to speak to me. Lowering his voice, he said: "George told me that you led the team across the field for his opening furrow *as straight as an arrow*. You know, coming from George, that is praise indeed". Without saying any more he picked up his bike and cycled off. Inwardly I was elated – he had made my day - I had achieved praise from George! All George's grumpiness was forgiven and I knew that it would never worry me again. We carried on ploughing until the usual time and then un-yoked for returning to the stable. We had simply continued round our opening furrows and I assume that the area we completed was sufficient for the purpose Harry required. This had been my last day with George, so whether subsequently he had to complete the whole of the small field I don't know; if he did he would have done it with the team abreast, working on his own.

We took the horses back to Impington Farm and after I had taken the harness off the mare, I spent much of the rest of my time grinding mangolds for feeding. This was a bigger job than it had been at Park Farm, because of the greater number of horses involved at this farm. Edgar, the head horseman had also returned to the stable with his team at about the same time as George and me, and while I was grinding the mangolds the two of them were busy making up the feeds. These feeds, composed of chaff, crushed oats and ground mangolds, were assembled in a circular sieve – which had wooden sides of about 4 inches high, and the bottom made of woven split cane. A brief shake of the sieve, before bringing it to the manger, would remove any dust from the feed. After about twenty minutes of our arrival other horsemen began coming into the stable with their horses and soon the whole place was buzzing with the sound of chatter and of harness being taken off and hung up.

When I had finished mangold grinding, I carried out the other daily routine of grooming the mare, meantime listening to the steady munching of all the horses. There was also the occasional clatter of horse shoes moving on the flat cobbled floor, as one of the men, having groomed one side of a horse, shoved him across so he could get between the horses to do the other side. So ended my last day of leading for 'Old George', at about the end of February or early March 1944.

In addition to Edgar and George, head horse-keeper and second horse-keeper respectively, there were a number of other horsemen who used to work with the Impington Farm horses. One man I later got to know quite well was Percy Bowers, a likeable man of about 50, of medium height and thick-set, but who had a rather unusual gait. Most people when they walk usually swing their arms to some extent, which moves their shoulders slightly backwards and forwards in the *opposite* direction to the legs of the same side. Percy did not appear to swing his arms at all. As his right leg came forward, his body would swing round with it, and likewise with the left side, which produced a relaxed-looking, but rather ungainly walk. This gave the impression that his body was too stiff for any twisting movement and therefore had to come round with each step in order to follow his legs. Percy was the only horseman on the farm who, when returning to the farm after work, instead of walking at the side of his horse, used to walk in front of it, with the horse's nose almost touching the back of his neck.

Impington Farm - Layout
This is a convenient point to give a rough description of Impington Farm, i.e. the farm-yard and its buildings. As you turned in off the Cambridge road, through the front wide gateway, with its pair of high and solid wooden gates, the first building on the left was a small wooden office for the use of the farm foreman, Harry Chambers. Beyond the office, still on the left and facing you end-on, were a pair of substantial semi-detached farm cottages; the first one the home of Harry; the second one the home of Edgar the farm's head horse-keeper. The front doors of the cottages were on the right-hand side, facing the

farmyard; their gardens were on the left-hand side and so were out of sight from the yard.

Some way beyond the cottages, still on the left and end on in the same line as the cottages, was a long cart hovel with an open front. Further still, again in the same line was a row of about six tall walnut trees. Returning to just inside the farm entrance and with your back to the gates, on your right, parallel to the public road outside, were two brick buildings; first a loose-box and beyond a long shed with a tool-loft above it. Access to the loft was by way of an outside heavy wooden ladder leading up to a door on the front of the building. Beyond these, also continuing parallel to the road was a six or seven foot high wall extending, I would guess, for about thirty or so yards.

At the far end of the above wall, and extending to its left at right angles, was a long brick building with a large door in the middle of the front wall, which now faces you as you look across from the farm gateway. This was the stable. Continuing in the same line to the left, and end-on to the stable, was a large wooden barn, and beyond that a smaller wooden construction that was the mangold store. Moving now, with your back to the front wall along the public road – extending across to the left, at right angles to the mangold store, was a long open fronted shelter with a pantiled roof. This same shelter then extended at right angles to *its* left, and continued back towards you and the front farmyard wall you have your back to. The near end of this shelter stopped about twenty feet short of the front corner of the building beneath the tool loft, the remaining distance being closed off with a wooden fence with a five-barred gate in the middle. It will be seen that the wall, the buildings and the fence just described, enclose quite a large area. This yard and the open fronted shelter was strawed down for use of the horses overnight during the winter period. A water trough was situated alongside the fence to one side of the five-barred gate.

Behind the straw-yard and the above shelter just described, at the rear of the farm, was another smaller yard, with three or four loose-boxes along one side. These boxes were where the farm ponies were stabled.

27

Behind this was a meadow that was used for turning the horses into at night during the summer time.

Carting Straw
(Photograph courtesy of the Cambridgeshire Collection)

A Load of Hay and Younger Company
One very cold and frosty morning I arrived at the farm gates a little
before 7 am. and waited with the other men who were assembling there,
for Harry to come out and give his orders for the day. Having spent
just over two months leading the plough horses, I was looking forward
to a change, but wondering just what this might be. When it came to
my turn, Harry told me that he wanted me to help Douglas Plumb to
fetch a load of hay. He didn't give any more details but indicated that
Douglas knew all about it. Now Douglas was one of the current 'pony
boys', so it seemed that I was to get in on the act of pony-lorry driving
– or at least as the driver's mate – which sounded quite an acceptable
change from being with George.

Pleased with the new assignment, I parked my bike under one of the
cart hovels at the rear of the farm and then looked out for Douglas. He
arrived on his bike shortly after and I told him that I was to be his mate.
He said that, yes, he knew – Harry had told him the previous day when
he had left off work. We walked round to the loose-box where
Douglas's brown pony was housed. The top half of the door was open
and, as we approached, I could see that the pony was standing normally
with its nose over its manger at the back of the box. Being used to the
stolid and calm reaction of the horses in the stable, I was surprised to
see what happened next. When Douglas opened the lower section of
the door and went in the pony immediately swung its rear end round
towards him and wouldn't let him near its head. He tried two or three
more times, with the same result, before the pony relented and let him
up alongside, to harness it up. He told me that this was a regular
morning ritual with this particular pony, but that it always gave up in
the end – in all other ways it was perfectly normal and obedient.

When Douglas was ready we walked back round to the hovel, and he
harnessed the pony between the shafts of his lorry. The wooden buck
of the lorry was about 14 feet long by 7 feet wide. It had an upright
section of about 30 inches high across the front, with a seat for the
driver on top and in the middle of this section, plus a footrest below. A
brake handle at the side of the seat, acted on the two rear wheels. The
other two lorries in use on the farm were of a very similar design and

size. Before we set off I asked Douglas whether he thought we would be back at the farm for breakfast. He said that we would definitely not be back by then and we had better take our dockey bags with us.

When we set off Douglas stood behind the seat to drive rather than sitting on the seat, as it was so cold – with me standing beside him. We came out of the farm gate and turned right onto the Cambridge Road. I asked where we were going and Douglas told me the name of a place which I have now forgotten. I remember we skirted the edge of Cambridge before getting out into the countryside again. I think we possibly took the Coton direction and our destination could have been Hardwick. I was aware that Chivers had a number of other farms, in addition to those in the immediate vicinity of Histon, though on this occasion we did not actually call at a farmyard, but to a large haystack in a corner of a field. Douglas had been there recently and knew where to find it.

It was a nice dry morning, though still freezing cold. Had I been still leading for George, the constant walking would have warmed me up, but now standing still on the lorry the low temperature was much more keenly felt. However, the atmosphere this morning was completely different and their was nothing icy about the conversation as we youngsters laughed and joked with each other. I remember coming out with the rhyme: "Oh Mr. Chivers – I shivers!", which made Douglas laugh. He was a very tall young chap, at least six feet I would guess, and I was conscious of this difference in height as we stood side by side on the lorry, with the pony clip-clopping along the road. The frost had made the road icy in places and once or twice the pony tended to slip a little, so instead of the usual trotting with the empty lorry, Douglas was content with a smart walk.

Our journey must have taken us at least seven or eight miles and it was almost 9 o'clock, breakfast time, before we arrived at the field that Douglas was aiming for. It was a grass field and the haystack stood in one corner, not far from the gateway. I got down from the lorry, feeling a bit stiff with the cold, and opened the gate; closing it again behind him after he had pulled into the field. Happily, there was now a little weak sunshine trying to come through, which, although unable to make much difference to the temperature, did make everything around pleasantly bright. Perhaps it was the psychological effect of this that decided us to have our breakfast on the bright side of the stack.

Leaving the pony nearby, with his leader dropped, we made ourselves comfortable, sitting on folded sacks with our backs to the stack and looking out across the field. During breakfast, Douglas asked me how I had liked working with Old George. He had never worked with George himself, but he knew that none of the other boys liked being with him. I told him that I wasn't keen myself, but that as time had gone on I had learned how to react to George and things had improved. There was a bit more of conversation but we didn't spend too much time over breakfast; having got thoroughly chilled on the way here, we were now keen to start moving in order to warm up.

The haystack, I noticed, although it had been started on, had not been cut from one end with a stack-knife. Instead the removed hay had obviously been taken from the top, across the whole stack, and had then been covered by a large tarpaulin to protect it from the weather. The tarpaulin had been weighted down by a long ladder tied below one edge, and a long heavy pole below the other; on the opposing long sides of the stack. To prevent the hanging edges of the sheet blowing up, ladder and pole were further secured by stakes, driven at an angle, into the stack. After removing the weights, Douglas used the ladder to climb the stack. He pulled up the tarpaulin, folded it up as best he could and left it to one side on the stack. He explained that as the cover was heavy, this was easier than pulling it right off and then having to haul it up again later.

If I had had previous experience of loading hay it would have been sensible for Douglas to have stayed where he was on the stack, and for me to start loading the lorry. As things were, he suggested that he start the loading and we would change over part way. Douglas came down from the stack, drew the pony alongside it, jumped onto the lorry and picked up one of the two-tined forks we had brought with us. Meanwhile I climbed the ladder to the top of the stack, with my fork ready to throw hay down to the lorry. Now, on the previous occasion when hay had been removed, before the tarpaulin had been replaced, a rounded mound of loose hay had been placed beneath it in order to shed any rain. This loose hay was easily dealt with and thrown down to Douglas. But then it became more difficult to 'find' each forkful. After a stack of hay or straw is built, it gradually settles down and the original loose stuff becomes greatly compressed under the weight of the mass of material. It then becomes a more skilled job to be able to 'see' how the hay is laid and to get your fork into a top piece, rather than tugging at lower pieces tightly held in.

Douglas stood on the lorry ready for loading and I started to throw the hay down to him from the stack, carefully aiming my forkfuls to land *just in front of him.* I had learned the need for this deliberate 'placing' of the material being loaded a few years earlier, when I had helped to pitch sheaves on the Bamford's farm during harvest time. If you placed the material properly in front of the loader it made his job so much easier – it is annoying, and much harder work, for the loader to continually have to retrieve the material from behind him. The movement of gathering the forksful of hay and throwing them down was enjoyable; I began to get warmer and before long took off my top coat. Previously, with the frost and the inactivity during the ride from Histon I had needed the coat, but now it was nice to discard it and to enjoy a bit of action.

After we had worked for some time, Douglas said that he thought he now had about half a load, and would I come down to see how straight it was. I climbed down the ladder and looked all round the lorry to judge the straightness of the sides of his load. I told him that they looked quite good. He suggested that we change jobs, which would give me opportunity to try my hand at loading, so we changed over. I moved the ladder round to the side of his load so that he could get down, and we changed places on the load; Douglas went up to take my place on the stack. Not having loaded any loose hay before I wondered whether I would be able to keep the sides straight; I decided to try to follow the system I had seen Charlie Bamford use when he was loading sheaves of corn (see 'Boy on a Branch' page 92).

32

We re-commenced loading and very soon I had to ask Douglas to go a little slower; his forks-full were coming down too thick and fast for me to handle. He slowed up and I got on a lot better. I carefully positioned good forks-full of hay round the edges of the load, then tied them in with overlapping ones within, and lastly good-sized lumps along the middle. This seemed to work fairly well and I was reasonably confident that I was managing to keep a straight-up load. Eventually Douglas came down from the stack to have a look and told me that it looked pretty good, and that he thought with a bit more across the middle we would have enough. After he'd thrown down the required amount, which I spread across the middle of the load, he came down again and said: "Hold tight, I'm going to draw the lorry away from the stack so as to give us room to rope the load down". I was rather concerned at this but knelt down and braced myself by grabbing hold of my fork, which I had jammed down hard in front of me into the hay. Douglas inched the lorry clear of the stack without mishap.

The next job was to secure the load with the lorry rope, which Douglas took from the hook where it hung on the off-side front of the buck-board. He attached the rope to a hook on the near-side of the lorry, a short distance from the rear end, and then threw the rest of the coiled rope up to me on top of the load. "Keep the end of the rope on top of the load" he said, "but throw me down a loop on the off-side". I did this, and after he'd pulled the rope tight across the rear of the load and fastened it on the off-side, he asked me to take the rope diagonally towards the front and to drop down a further loop near the near-side front. This he fastened on that front hook. After that, the rope was taken over the front of the load, tightened, and fastened on the off-side front hook, before being taken across diagonally to the near-side rear. Thus, the load was neatly secured with a rope side to side across back and front, plus diagonally back to front on both sides.

Douglas placed the ladder against the load for me to descend to terra firma and reminded me that we still had the stack to re-cover. We both climbed onto the stack and heaped some hay across the middle to make the surface slightly convex, before pulling the tarpaulin over once more. We hung the ladder on one side and the heavy pole on the other, on the strings attached to the edges of the cover, and made all secure. We sat down alongside the stack in the sunshine, which had become a bit stronger and feeling measurably warmer, and had some drinks from our thermos flasks.

When we were ready to set off back we realised we had a slight problem. Douglas had arranged a space round the driving seat when he'd loaded the hay, but there was not enough room for two and I would have to ride on top of the load. However, without untying the ladder again, it would be difficult to get up there. Not wanting to bother with the ladder, Douglas gave me a leg-up part way and I managed to pull myself up the rest of the way on one of the ropes. I stowed our two forks by laying them on top with the tines sticking into the hay and the handles beneath a rope. Douglas shouted that he was ready to go and warned me to hang on for the uneven ground in the gateway. Feeling rather insecure perched on top of the load, I decided the safest thing would be to lie down along the middle and hold on to the diagonal ropes, one in each hand. The load swayed a bit, though not too alarmingly as Douglas led the pony out onto the road. Then, when he had shut the field gate and settled himself in his seat, we started back towards Histon. I decided to stay as I was, laying on my back. With the smoothness of the hard road and the clip-clop of the pony's hooves I was soon lulled into a reverie and it was a very relaxing ride. A strange thought – to be paid for two hours of resting in the hay!

The hay was required, Douglas had told me, not for the horses but for the cows at Cawcutt's Farm. On reaching Impington Farm on our left, we continued about a further half a mile and turned right into Cawcutt's Farm roadway and down to the farm at the end of the road. It was after 1.30 pm when we arrived at the farm, and Douglas said that he was famished. I had eaten one of my sandwiches on the way, but it had not been convenient for Douglas to eat whilst wedged in the hay and driving the pony, so he decided now that the first thing to do was to have our dockey; which we did. Afterwards it didn't take very long to unload the hay into the hay store, with Douglas throwing it down from the lorry and me forking it into the store. One of the cowmen came round to the store to inspect the hay, and after a chat with him we trotted back to Impington Farm. We met Harry at the farm; he sent Douglas off on a short errand with the pony and told me that I could spend the rest of the afternoon grinding some mangolds for the horses. So ended a relaxing and enjoyable day.

The Tumbrel Cart

Tumbrel carts were a sort of 'Jack of all trades' cart. They were used for carting farmyard manure, coal, roots: e.g. mangolds for stock-feed; loose potatoes, e.g. when carting off the field; bagged potatoes, and all sorts of other things. In some parts of the country they were known as a 'tip cart'. All in all they were a very useful form of agricultural conveyance (this is not the place to go into the use they were put to in the French Revolution!).

The Chivers' tumbrels were of sturdy wooden construction, had a square body of about 5 feet each way, with front and sides of about 30 inches high. The back- board was hinged at the bottom so that it could be let down to open the back of the cart. The body itself could be tipped right back until the rear end was virtually touching the ground. Alternatively it could be held partly tipped by means of a chain at the front. The body was kept in its normal position, or tipped, by means of a handle at the end of a metal slide. The slide was located across the shafts just behind the horse and kept in place by metal retaining clips and pin. A heavy wooden axle frame extended across the underneath of the cart, attached to which on iron stubs were the two high, iron-tyred wheels, reaching almost to the top of the cart sides. A board attached along the top of the sides extended outwards about 9 inches above the wheels.

Farmyard Manure Carting

I had two separate sessions of manure carting, or *'muck carting'*, as we used to call it, and the loads were treated differently at the delivery site on the two occasions. Whether these two bouts of carting were in different years I cannot now recall, but I will describe them both. It would have been in early April I think, and the cows at Cawcutts Farm had been turned out to graze. The large cattle yards, which had accommodated the dairy cows during the past winter were to be cleared of the tons of manure that had accumulated.

The manure was to be carted from the yards to a field that lay at some distance on the far side of the main Histon-Cambridge road. The route, as I remember it, was in a fairly straight line: down to the end of the Cawcutt's farm road, to the main road, then straight across this and onto another farm roadway on the far side. This then continued for quite a way to the field to which the manure was to be taken. Tumbrel carts were used for the carting, each one holding about one ton. The manure was removed from the rear, via the drop-down back-board. The work was organised by the foreman rather like a military operation, in order that none of the men and boys involved should be held up at any stage and so waste time.

On this occasion the manure was to be unloaded into heaps in the field, for later spreading by hand. An experienced man would be stationed in the field to remove the one ton load into two or three heaps at regular intervals which must be at the required spacing for applying the tonnage per acre which had been decided upon. If we assume that each tumbrel took him 15 minutes to unload, also that leading the horse and loaded tumbrel from the cattle yard to the destination field, took 20 minutes, then another 20 minutes to return to the yard, that is a time of 55 minutes between the loading and the return of one cart. Assuming also, that it takes the two men stationed in the yard 15 minutes to load the cart, then if only one tumbrel was employed for the carting, 55 minutes between each load would be lost by each of the three men. The foreman has to determine how many tumbrels, and boys to lead them, he will need to keep everyone busy.

Exactly how many carts and boys were used on this particular day I cannot remember, except that I was one of the boys. It must have taken all of Harry's good judgement to get the organisation about right so that the men were not kept unoccupied for too long at a time. Having said that, loading trodden muck from a yard into a tumbrel is hard work; so is unloading the tumbrel in the field, by pulling it out of the cart with a muck-crome, especially if the ground is sticky to walk on. All three men deserve a short breather in between – something else for Harry to include in his calculations! At least, we boys got an inevitable 15 minute break at each end of the route, whilst we watched the loading and unloading going on. It would have been difficult for Harry to have found us anything useful to do during these breaks.

Leading the horses between the yard and field was quite straightforward, though you had to be careful to watch for traffic before crossing the main road, though its volume in no way approached the volume of today, 2008. One other thing to adhere to was the farm precept: '*Loaded Carts Go First*'. When on the way with a loaded cart you would pass other boys returning with empty ones. Now, whilst the Cawcutt's Farm roadway was quite wide, the farm road on the opposite side of the main road was only of single cart width. When two carts met here, one had to give way and move over to the headland at the side of the road and, if conditions were sticky it was not very wise to take the loaded cart into the mud. If possible we would look out for the dryer spots and try to pass there.

On the other occasion when I had the same job of 'muck carting' instead of the manure being carted straight out onto the field, it was built into a large muck-heap, or midden. The reason for stacking it, I suppose, would either have been that the field where it was wanted was not yet clear for ploughing; or, it was not required to be used until autumn. On some farms, when manure is stacked, it is tipped out of the cart, then subsequent loads are backed up to the heap as it progresses and some of the material is thrown on top of the tipped stuff. As there is a limit to how high it can be thrown, the heap gets extended in length and area and is left relatively loose, which tends to allow its nutrients to leach more easily. On the one occasion when I saw it stacked in a field at Chivers, the manure was consolidated rather than being left loose; in fact the operative word is the one I used above: the heap was '*built*'.

I must have been put on the job of leading the horses and manure tumbrels on this particular occasion a day, or a couple of days, after it had been commenced. When I arrived at the site with my first load I found that there was already a massive heap in place. It had already reached a height of about 4 feet; it was circular in form and looking quite solid; the top was fairly flat and on one edge of its circumference, the manure had been formed into a wide ramp from the ground up to the top. On entering the field I was met by a man and a horse. The man was Walter Coxall[2] from Park Farm and his horse had trace gears on.

Walter hooked on his horse to the front of my tumbrel; then, guiding the reins of the trace horse with his left hand he took my horse from me with his right hand. As I looked on, astonished, he drove the team and the cart up the left-hand side of the ramp of the muck-heap. It was quite a stiff pull, but the horses pulled the load to the top. Then, as I watched I almost had kittens: Walter, keeping the trace horse over to the left, drove the team round the circumference of the heap with the leading horse so near the edge that I expected to see him topple over any second. I thought that I had never seen anything as skilfully done as those two horses being driven round on top of the midden. Walter stopped the horses at a point he had decided on, and tipped the manure out of the cart. The team and cart were then driven round the rest of the circle and back down the ramp. After a short chat with Walter, I left the field with the empty cart. As I looked back Walter was busy with his fork, levelling the load he had just tipped.

More Carting Jobs
One morning Harry sent me on my bike, to the carpenters' shop at the factory with three or four pruning saws to be sharpened. I was to wait for them to be done, and then to return them to the pruners. By the time I had done this and got back to the farm it was almost breakfast time, so I had my breakfast in a mess-hut at the back of the farmyard. Breakfast at the farm was unusual, for normally I was working elsewhere at breakfast time. After breakfast Harry told me that he wanted me to collect a tumbrel load of coal from Histon station, and he explained how to find the coal bay in the station yard.

---

[2] *This was definitely the horseman from Park Farm, but see earlier Note 1 concerning his name.*

There was only one horse left in the stable, a large white mare, so I harnessed her up with her cart harness and went round to the cart hovel. I chose a cart that had been left by the previous user with the cart tipped and the shafts pointing upwards, with the ridge chain still in place. The mare was then backed under the shafts which were pulled down to the sides of the horse, whilst carefully placing the ridge, or supporting chain, in the groove in the cart saddle. It was then a simple matter to attach the rest of the harness to the shafts: the tug chains at the front and breeching chains at the back. Finally, the belly-band under the horse, attached from one shaft to the other and which prevented the cart from tipping up.

When we were ready I stood in the cart and drove out of the farm and along the public road to Histon station. I suppose that on arrival, I must have had to report to the goods yard office and also possibly have the horse and cart weighed on a weigh-bridge, though I cannot now remember any of these details. All I now recall is the actual loading of the coal. The cart was backed up to the coal bay, and then it was a case of shovelling the coal into the cart. For a start the back-board was lowered so that the coal did not have to be thrown too high. It was thrown towards the front until as much as possible was loaded without any falling out of the back. When this was achieved, the back-board was raised again and the remainder of the load had to be thrown over the top. Some of the coal was in such large lumps that I found it easier to pick these up by hand, rather than use the shovel. I loaded as much as possible with the load heaped up, but was careful about the distribution. A tumbrel is designed with the wheels in the middle of the body and, if care is taken with the loading, it can be extremely well balanced. Loaded with rather more weight towards the front, so that there is a bit of downward pressure on the cart saddle, is the most comfortable for the horse.

I took the load of coal back to Impington Farm, but did not have to unload it; this was taken over by someone else and I was given another job. I think the coal was probably intended for the fires of the two farm cottages. Still on the subject of coal, at leaving off time that day, I saw something that I had never heard of, either then or since. As I walked towards the farm exit with my bike, two or three of the farm staff were looking over the stable door into the loose-box to the left of the gate. One of them said: "Come and look at these", so I went across to look. Inside were about half a dozen young pigs, gathered round a little heap of what looked like coal dust. They were picking out the larger pieces and busily crunching them up. Presumably the coal had been collected from the bottom of the cart after my load had been emptied. On enquiring the reason for the pigs being given the coal, I was told that they were able to get various minerals from it. I have looked at a number of books on pig keeping, but have never come across mention of this practice since. I do not remember any sow being with them, so whether the pigs were orphaned, or were weaners I don't know.

All Steamed Up
Another carting job – which is engraved on my memory, was to take some seed corn to where Edgar, the head horse-keeper, was drilling. At least, that was the intention – I did not arrive there. The seed was contained in paper sacks, which probably indicated that it had been purchased rather than being farm-saved seed. The location of the field where the drilling was taking place was some distance from the farm, through a number of fruit orchards, past the 'Nursery' and 'Big' sheds previously mentioned, and out to the arable fields beyond. This route, though, is rather academic so far as I am concerned for, as I said, on this occasion I did not get there.

Normally a few sacks of this nature would have been delivered by one of the pony lorries, but presumably one was not available when I was asked to take the seed. Instead, I took one of the tumbrel carts, placed the bags of seed in that, and set off along the Cambridge Road. I had walked along the public road with the horse but, after turning right onto the farm road, I decided to ride. Not bothering to make room to stand in the cart among the sacks, I sat instead on the near-side front of the cart, with my feet resting on the rear of the shaft. Continuing along this straight piece of road, on the left-hand side was a fairly deep ditch. On the far side of the ditch was a large arable field that stretched back across to the Cambridge Road.

I jogged along the road in a relaxed frame of mind, and then spotted a steam engine working on the far side of the field, with a queer-looking object creeping towards it from within the field. Another engine stood at rest just across the ditch a little way ahead of me. I had never before seen a steam-ploughing team at work – which this was – otherwise I would have been prepared for what happened next. In my ignorance of the set-up, I had not realised that the large piece of equipment across the field was a six-furrow plough that the far engine had pulled towards it across the field, on a cable. Now, of course, quite unexpected by me, the nearer engine across the ditch suddenly, with a belch of smoke, noisily started working to pull the plough back to the near side of the field.

It was not just me who was startled by the engine – taken by surprise, the horse was terrified. He flung himself away from the ditch and the noisy thing on the other side of the ditch and started to back the cart at the same time. I yelled 'Whoa' to the horse but he took no notice and continued to back away. With a horse bolting forwards there is a chance of pulling him up with the reins; but with one going backwards, the reins are useless. Jumping down from the cart as fast as I could I rushed to hold the horse's head to try to straighten him up, but I was too late. The near-side cart wheel went over the edge of the ditch and started rolling down the side. Suddenly the horse realised that he was no longer going back by his own volition, but was being *pulled* backwards. He now tried to stop the cart, but too late; the backward momentum continued too fast for him and I could do nothing to stop him. With the oblique angle of the cart, I had visions of both cart and horse collapsing over sideways down into the ditch. All I managed to do before both of the large wheels were resting in the bottom of the ditch, was to pull the horse round square.

It now felt that I had landed in a serious predicament: the cart was well and truly stuck in the ditch. However the horse, my main concern, was now stretched out with his hind feet down in the ditch and the front ones resting on the edge of the bank. Furthermore, he was still tightly harnessed to the cart and the shafts were pressing down on his back.

41

He seemed to be completely immobilised. I stood on the bank appalled at the situation I had got into. I wondered whether I could possibly get down alongside the horse to undo his harness, which looked unlikely as all its chains were now pulled taught by the weight of the cart. The horse himself provided the solution: with a sudden shudder and a terrific effort he strained, broke free from the harness, and managed to climb out of the ditch. I grabbed him by the bridle rein, wondering what he would now do, but he now stood quietly with no more fuss. I was worried as to whether he had sustained any injuries, but as far as I could see he appeared to be unharmed.

I stood holding the horse and pondered what I should do next – the only thing for it, I thought was to take the horse back to the farm and let Harry know of my embarrassing accident. Before I could act on this decision, however, I saw Harry turn the corner at the end of the road and cycle towards me, so I stood and waited for him, feeling very uneasy. It felt very undignified standing there with the horse and with the cart shafts sticking up in the air above the edge of the ditch. It must, on first sight, have looked odd to Harry as he approached us, but I expect that when he saw the steam-plough on the other side of the ditch he probably was able to assess the situation immediately. *"Hello"* said Harry, *"are you in the ditch?"* Now normally I was a diffident boy, but being rather worked up about what I'd done, I was surprised to hear myself answer: *"It looks like it doesn't it"*. I had never heard Harry swear, but at the very least I had expected a severe telling off – but all Harry said was: *"Well, I'll go to Hanover"*.

We took a look at the cart and from what we could see, it didn't appear to have been damaged. The bags of seed corn had been shot down into the rear of the cart and I could see that one of them had burst open and the seed scattered between the bags. Harry said that he would get the Italian prisoners to come and remove the seed and to get the cart out of the ditch. He asked me to walk the horse backwards and forwards for a short distance, while he stood and checked that he was satisfied that no damage had been done to him. Meantime I was hoping that my mistake would not result in Harry taking me off working with the horses, for I was becoming very attached to them. I was therefore much relieved when, after deciding that the horse was OK, he ordered me to take him back to the stable and change his harness ready for horse-hoeing. I was then to start horse-hoeing in the strawberries.

Subsequently, I heard that 'Curly' had given the six or seven Italian prisoners a lift to the site. They had passed the bags of seed corn up to Curly's lorry and he had delivered them to the men who were drilling. I imagine that there were enough of the Italians to work the cart up the sides of the ditch and pull it out. One consolation was that there had been very little water in the ditch; had the water been deep then the paper sacks of seed would have become a soggy mess; as it was they stayed clear of the water within the cart. Thus ended my ignominious excursion with the seed corn. I tried to put the episode behind me and spent the rest of the day horse-hoeing.

Keeping the Strawberries 'Clean'
As instructed by Harry after the above steam-plough incident, I took the horse back to the farm to change his harness ready for horse-hoeing. As I removed his cart harness I was disturbed to find that some parts of it were damaged – chain links snapped and stitching pulled undone on some of the leather-work. It was obviously going to need some repairs and I could imagine the caustic comments I would probably receive when Edgar, the head horse-keeper would see it later. The damage had obviously been done when the horse had made that terrific effort to free himself, when he was down in the ditch. I had been so relieved at the lack of damage to the horse, that I had failed to notice that to the harness. Surprisingly, I never heard a word about it from Edgar; I could only assume that Harry had perhaps explained the situation to him and he had made allowances for my inexperience.

Having changed the harness I left the farm once more with the horse, and made my way to the strawberry field. The horse-hoe had already been delivered there and stood in the corner of the field. This implement had a small wheel in the middle at the front and, behind the wheel, joined to each other by a hinge, were two horizontal sides of a metal frame. This frame extended back about 4 feet behind the wheel and had an attachment at the rear by which the width between the two sides could be narrowed or widened as required, thus forming a horizontal, elongated triangle. At the rear were two handles for the operator, rather like plough handles. Attached along the side frames, at about 12 or 14 inch intervals, were metal legs with hoe blades at the bottom, and a single leg between the two at the front. This arrangement enabled the whole width between the frame to be covered by the blades; also, different row widths of crops could be catered for by means of the width adjustment at the rear of the frame.

The row width of the strawberries, I would guess, would be about 3 feet. Before starting the horse-hoeing, the field would have been gone over by a gang of men using hand hoes. The strawberry plants would be hand hoed between them and along their sides. As the hoeing progressed, a little soil would be drawn towards the plants on each side – which treatment, I understand, encourages them to make fresh roots higher up their crowns. The role of the *horse-hoe* is then to cover the intervening space in the rows between that covered by the hand hoeing, taking care not to work too close to the plants and thus disturb the roots. This requirement, of course, is taken care of by adjusting the working width of the implement, as described above.

I yoked the horse to the front of the hoe and started off along the first row at one end of the field. At the far headland, instead of trying to come back down the adjacent row, which entails a very tight turn with the horse and hoe, I turned in an easier arc to enter a row a little further across. At the far end of this row, having gained the extra space for turning, it was then easy to turn into the row adjacent to the one I had started on, and so continue in this fashion across the field. The horse-hoe, I found, was a fairly stable piece of equipment; with a reliable horse who knew he should walk along the middle of the row, it was easy to handle and to keep in a straight line. If you got off line occasionally, say too much to the right, a slight downward pressure on that side handle would take you back again – and vice versa when too much the other way. The horse-hoe, when first used, needed a bit of practice to get used to, but I don't think that it needed anything like the skill required for ploughing.

I spent the rest of that day happily moving up and down the strawberry field, slicing through the weeds between the rows and making a nice shallow tilth. This tilth, I was told, helped with moisture retention. The next day continued in the same way, using the same horse, but on the following day Harry must have been short of a horse to cover all the jobs. When I arrived for work that morning, I was rather dismayed to be told by Harry to harness up who he called "the old white pony" – but who everybody else on the farm referred to as "the old dead pony". The pony really was quite old and was supposed to be in her retirement – I believe that she was about 35 years old – and I didn't think that she should be made to work. However, I did as Harry had directed and harnessed her up. She was well fed, I knew, but very skinny and I was ashamed to be seen walking her along the main road with working harness on.

On arrival at the field I yoked the pony to the hoe and started off working, but it was not long before the pony was struggling. Her wind was bad, coming in noisy gasps at each step and she sounded more like a steam engine than a pony. Watching the exertions of her poor old legs, and listening to her stertorous breathing made me feel bad. Unlike the horse, who had pulled the hoe effortlessly at a steady pace, the pony seemed that she had to struggle on at a faster pace in order to keep going and soon she was sweating profusely. I stopped and adjusted the hoe to a slightly shallower depth to make things a little easier for her, which helped a bit. It was the custom when carrying out horse operations to stop occasionally and give the horses a breather. Now, when I had turned in at the beginning of a row, I stopped and gave the poor old pony a rest for far longer than I had done for the horse – and unlike the horse, I gave the pony a rest at the beginning of *every* row. This meant that I was only covering a fraction of the work previously covered with the horse, and when Harry came he complained that I had not done very much. When I told him how I felt about the pony, and then showed him her pathetic efforts, I think he took the point. He said no more and cycled off again. He never asked me to take out the old 'dead pony' again.

Going to the Blacksmith
One enjoyable job that I was asked to do, on quite a number of occasions, was to take horses to the blacksmith for new shoes to be fitted. Chivers had their own blacksmith's shop at Impington. Impington was a next-door neighbour of Histon, and the two villages were virtually joined. Over a period of time I must, I think, have taken practically all the individual horses from the Impington Farm stable to have their feet attended to by the blacksmith. This was a job for the boys, as there was usually quite a bit of waiting time involved for which the men could not be spared. You had the choice as to whether you would lead the horse, or ride him to the smith's, as Harry seemed to have no objection to you having a ride. This could be either side-saddle or not, as the fancy took you – in any case the ride would be bare-back – but, assuming the weather was fine, always enjoyable.

Amongst the farm's horses I can remember are the following: Boxer, Punch, Rufus, Short, and Tom. For some strange reason I remember these as some of the horse's names, but cannot now recall those of the mares. The only horse I would *not ride* to the blacksmith's was Rufus. He was a dark coloured horse with flecks of a sort of red – hence, I suppose his name. Rufus, like all the other horses, was very good in traffic, *except* for his one great hate: *big red buses*. Of these he was terrified and, if you saw one coming you had to be prepared, for as the bus approached Rufus would attempt to jump away from it, straight off the side of the road. This habit did not lend itself to a wish to be on his bare back when he jumped; it was much more prudent to lead him and control him by holding him tight at his head.

Whether these visits to the blacksmith were pre-arranged by Harry, I don't know, but usually the 'smith would arrange to stop what he was doing to deal with the horse. With the periodic attention he gave to all the farms' horses, he got to know then fairly well, and the horses in their turn, were well accustomed to having their 'pedicures'. Occasionally when a horse felt a bit fractious the smith would ask you to hold it; you would stand at its head, hold its leader and talk to it quietly, which was usually enough to relax it. One horse, I remember, had a habit that intensely annoyed the blacksmith; this happened when he had lifted the horse's back foot and was holding it between his legs, ready to remove the old shoe. This crouched position, with the knees bent and holding the leg of the horse, was not a very comfortable posture – as I knew from my experience in the stable when inspecting a rear hoof – but this particular horse made the discomfort worse. He would actually *lean* on the side being held, thus putting a lot of weight on the poor blacksmith. You could imagine the horse thinking to himself: *"Ah, this is relaxing, I'll make the most of it"*. The blacksmith's reaction was to throw down the leg, hit him on the rump with the flat of his hammer, and shout: "Stand up!"

The blacksmith wore a thick leather apron, which had a perpendicular split in the lower part covering the thighs. I imagine that this heavy apron gave him good protection from scrapes and bruises in dealing with the horses' feet, but without the split in the bottom it would obviously have been too clumsy to be able to hold a hoof between his legs. Shoeing the horse was quite a skilled operation. The first stage was to remove the old shoes, which was done with a large pair of metal pincers. Starting at one end, the shoe was gripped and levered away from the hoof, continuing right round the shoe. Whilst this was done the hoof had to be gripped quite tightly in order to counteract the levering action of the pincers. Once the shoe was loosened all round, it was pulled away from the hoof, thus withdrawing all the old nails at the same time. This was then continued for each of the other three feet.

The next stage in the re-shoeing is trimming the feet. The hoof, basically, consists of the outer hard, solid looking part that can be seen as we look at the horse, and in the middle underneath is the frog, a softer part which gives a kind of cushioning effect as the horse walks or runs. The outer hoof continues to grow and for horses in the wild this growth takes care of the wear-and-tear involved in their running around. The *working* horse has metal shoes fitted to prevent the *over-much* wear that can occur when a horse is regularly working. However, in this case, the new growth to the hoof that has occurred between each visit to the blacksmith, does not get worn down, being protected by the shoes. Hence, when the old worn-out shoes are removed and before the new ones are fitted, the hoof needs trimming down to a suitable level with the special blacksmith's knife. Here again, the foot needs gripping tightly as this paring of the hoof takes place, and the skill of the blacksmith is seen as he pares the hoof down to a correct profile for receiving the new shoe.

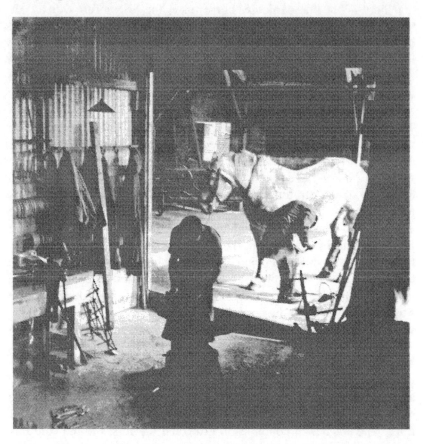

At the Blacksmith's
(Photograph courtesy of the Cambridgeshire Collection)

Next comes the fitting of the shoes. The smith will have already assessed the size of the hooves of the horse he is dealing with and will have had a shoe heating up in his forge. He knocks the end of a metal punch into one of the outer nail-holes in the shoe. This protruding punch acts as a handle for him to carry the red-hot shoe to the horse, where he places the shoe lightly on the pared-down hoof and checks the fit. Any slight final adjustment needed to the shoe is then dealt with by hammering it on his anvil. Then the heated shoe is once more placed and pressed onto the hoof, which burns the hoof down to the exact profile of the shoe, thus making a perfect fit. Whilst the hot shoe remains on the hoof, it produces a great deal of smoke and an extremely pungent smell from the burning hoof, which wafts up around the smith until he is almost hidden from sight. The smell, once experienced, is never forgotten!

Finally the cooled shoes are nailed on. The shoes are made with seven or eight holes through which the nails are inserted. On the outer, or 'underneath' side of the shoes (i.e. the sides of the shoes which rest on the ground) the nail-holes are made wider and square, in order to receive the special horse shoe nails, which have a square head. The nail-heads, when fitted, are able therefore to be recessed into the shoe, to lie almost flush with its outer surface. As with all the previous stages described, the 'smith has to pick up each foot between his legs to support them for nailing on the shoes. The nails, which are approximately 2 ½ - 3 inches in length, are inserted at a slight angle as they are hammered in, which directs them so that the ends emerge from the outside wall of the hoof about 2 inches high. The protruding nail ends are then removed, as near to the hoof as possible, by a deft twist in the claw of the blacksmith's hammer. The short pieces remaining after this, are clenched downwards with the hammer and nailed flush to the hoof.

I always enjoyed watching the skill of the blacksmith, and I think that the description given from memory above is reasonably accurate. When all four shoes have been fixed, the final touch is to smarten the hooves by brushing round them with a black oil. This job is usually passed over to the boy who had brought the horse. Then, after taking leave of the blacksmith, all that had to be done was to ride my smart horse, with his new shoes and shiny black feet, back to Impington Farm.

Park Farm Silo

When I had first worked at Park Farm I had noticed that standing at the side of the farmyard was a tall cylindrical concrete tower. I'd had no idea what its purpose was, or what it contained; however, when one day Harry sent me to assist Douglas on his pony lorry, I was to able to find out more about it. The tower, or 'silo' as it was called, contained silage which was used for cattle feeding, Douglas told me, and we were to take a load of this silage to Cawcutts for the cows. On arrival at Park Farm I had a closer look at the silo. Fixed to the outside of it was a metal pipe of about 6 to 8 inches diameter, which ran up the full height of the structure and then turned to enter the building at the top. This, I was told, was the filler pipe; a machine standing below it would chaff the material to be used and then blow it up the pipe to fill the silo. As the machine was not there, I assumed that it must have been a portable one that had been removed after use.

I was curious as to how you got into the silo to remove the silage; Douglas said: "If you look a bit further round, you'll find a metal ladder fixed up the outside of the wall." I looked, but there was no ladder to be seen and I realised that Douglas had been joking. We agreed that neither of us would feel very happy climbing up the outside – which would have been more suitable for a steeplejack! Then Douglas opened a wooden door in the concrete wall a little way round from the pipe, which I had not previously taken notice of, and I looked inside. There was indeed a metal ladder, attached to the inside wall of the building. This ladder, however, was enclosed in a sort of perpendicular concrete shaft, or tunnel, by means of an inner wall. This wall extending from the outside wall on one side of the ladder, round in a semicircle behind the ladder, to the wall on the other side. This left just enough space for climbing the ladder, but was close enough to the circular wall to be able to lean back on it. Being thus enclosed, the ladder was nothing like as formidable looking as a similar one on the outside would have been.

Douglas suggested that I go up into the silo to throw the silage down to him and he would load it onto the lorry. He told me that the silo was now down to about one-third full; also that when I climbed the ladder I would be able to see how I could get into the main chamber containing the silage. I did as he had suggested and began to climb the ladder. It was rather dim in the ladder shaft and the only light there was, seemed to be coming from the conical roof at the very top. This roof was either made of glass, or perhaps some kind of glass substitute. After climbing about a third of the way up, I came to an opening in the inner wall of the shaft, that was about 2 feet wide and 4 feet high. When I looked through this opening I could see the top of the silage just below its bottom edge, so I climbed through onto the silage.

After the dimness of the ladder shaft, I found that the light given by the roof-lights was much better in the main chamber. On looking up I found that the opening in the wall through which I had climbed in, was repeated by other similar openings at intervals right to the top; the height of wall between each gap would be roughly 4 feet, about the same as the height of the openings. All the openings, I noticed were able to be closed by means of wooden doors; the door of the opening by which I had entered, and all the doors above me had been pushed back to rest against the inner wall. These doors could be reached from the ladder shaft when next they needed to be closed again. The four-tined fork used for removing the silage, I found stuck in the top ready for me, as Douglas had said it would be. This avoided having to haul up a fork every time someone climbed the ladder.

The silage was forked across the chamber to the gap in the wall and then thrown down the ladder shaft. With the ground floor outer door open, a second man would remove it from where it landed at the bottom of the shaft. Care had to be taken whilst forking the material through the gap and into the shaft, to drop it as close as possible to the inner wall so that it fell clear of the ladder on the outer wall. On reflection, I think that the design of the silo, enabling the efficient handling of the material, was quite clever. My throwing down of the silage took rather less time than it did for Douglas to load it and level it on the lorry, and it wasn't long before there was quite a heap waiting to be moved.

As I didn't know how much more would be required to make up the load, I left off forking and went down the ladder to talk to Douglas. The heap of silage in the restricted space at the bottom of the ladder was quite high, so I couldn't get out to see how he was doing. Instead, I called to him through the small space between the heap and the top of the doorway. Douglas, ever ready to play a joke, said: " I think I've got enough on the load now – I won't bother with any more now, so I will get going; see you later." I then heard the clop of the pony moving on the concrete outside and I half thought that he meant what he said. However, in reality he was simply turning the lorry round to make it easier to load the other side. Having had to load up on his own, it had been easier to do it one side at a time. It didn't take him very long to clear the heap in the doorway and then, after the forking down of a little more silage, the load was completed and we took it to the cows at Cawcutts Farm.

Incidentally, the cows at Cawcutts were all Jerseys; pedigree ones I think. Two Jersey bulls were also kept and these often used to be tethered on a grass area at the back of the farm-yard. The tethering equipment consisted of a metal rod of about 8 feet long, which rested on the ground and was hinged at one end by means of a metal stake driven into the ground. A chain from the ring in the bulls' nose was attached to the other end of the rod. The bull was thus able to walk in an 8 or 9 feet diameter circle, which afforded it some exercise.

The Water Carts
We had two water carts on the farm, a big one and a smaller one, but how many gallons of water they each carried I don't know. The first job I remember doing with one of these was the carrying of water to supply the big spray-tank, used in the orchards by the spraying gang. This spray-tank was a long square-sectioned tank, on a metal frame and with small metal wheels. It had a metal draw-bar at the front, used by the farm tractor driver to move it from place to place. The chemicals used for the spraying were mixed in the water in the spray tank, and the pressure to supply the lances being used by the men was produced by an engine on the machine. With three or four men spraying, quite a lot of water was required and this is where I came in with the water cart.

The orchards, as previously described were 'down the fen', in the vicinity of the 'Nursery' and the 'Big' sheds. The water had to be collected from Cawcutts Farm so was a fair distance away, taking about 25 minutes each way for the journey.

The water cart itself was of quite simple construction. Basically it was a large circular metal drum mounted on an iron frame, with large diameter metal wheels, and shafts at the front for a horse to pull it. The lid through which it was filled was located at the top, and it had a tap at the bottom at the rear, to which a length of hose could be attached. To have to fill the tank using an ordinary tap and small hose would be very time-consuming; instead, a special filler was used, located under an open fronted shed at Cawcutts Farm. The filler pipe in the shed was fixed above the height of the water carts, with a downward bend at the end. The diameter of this pipe was such that a large volume of water could be obtained quite quickly. You backed the cart under the shed, positioning it so that the hole in the top of the tank was immediately under the end of the pipe. Then, standing on the wheel-hub at the side of the cart you could turn on the tap by its circular wheel, and watch the water fill to a suitable level in the tank. It paid to ensure that positioning was exact; if not, you could find yourself in receipt of a hefty splash!

The men doing the spraying, which was a most unpleasant job, used to cut heavy sacks open so that they could use them to put over their heads and shoulders, to protect them somewhat from the sprays. I remember carting water for the sprayers on only this one occasion, but I do remember that it was an all-day job and I was backwards and forwards with no let-up, in order to be able to keep them going. This particular instance would have been in the springtime, I think. There was another time of water carting I remember which I think took place later in the year, probably about October. A field of cabbages had just been planted with young plants and I had to take the water-cart along the rows, stopping every so far, whilst someone at the rear watered each plant by means of a hose-pipe attached to the tap. I see from the diary I kept in 1947 that I did some other jobs with the water cart. However, as those diary entries are given in Part 2, I will leave any further notes concerning the water cart until then.

The Early Potatoes
The first step in the production of potatoes was the preparation of the ground in the autumn. An application of farmyard manure would be carted out onto the field from the manure heap, leaving it in equally spaced heaps containing sufficient manure to provide about 15 tons per acre. (see note of this under 'Carting Farmyard Manure'). The heaps would then be spread by hand, using four-tined manure forks, by some of the general farm workers. I have seen the manure being spread but this is a job I was never given whilst at Chivers. This manure would both feed the potatoes and help them with its moisture holding ability. In addition, a little artificial manure would be applied in the spring, when the potatoes were planted. After the farmyard manure was spread it would be ploughed in, by the ploughmen and their horses.

The next stage would be the arrival of the 'seed' potatoes. The ideal size of these is about the size of a hen's egg and they are required in quantities of about 15 hundred-weights for every acre to be grown. They would normally be 'Scotch' seed, arriving by rail in 1 cwt hessian sacks during January or February. Harry told me that the reason for using Scotch seed was that lowland potatoes were susceptible to various virus diseases, which the ones grown in the higher altitudes of Scotland were able to avoid. In general, therefore, the Scotch seed was more vigorous and produced a healthier crop. It was permissible, Harry said, to use farm-saved seed *once* from a crop produced from Scotch seed; this was known as *'once-grown Scotch seed'* and usually gave good results. However, to save your own seed on the farm for more than this one year, was asking for trouble, Harry said.

As soon as possible after arrival, the seed was taken out of the sacks, and put in single layers in special wooden potato trays. The dormant buds, or 'eyes', from which the sprouts grow, are mainly at one end of the tuber, known as the 'rose' end; so this end is kept upwards as far as possible. The trays have a raised handle at each end which, when the trays were 'stacked' gave about a 3 inch gap between each one in order to let light in from the sides. They then needed stacking in a frost free, light and airy place in order for the 'chitting' or sprouting of the seed to take place. It had been found that seed that had been chitted before planting, produced rather heavier crops; also if planting had to be delayed owing to bad weather, the chitted seed started off with the advantage that the sprouts were ready to grow immediately. Potato growers in the big potato growing districts, I understand, often place their trays of seed in glass-houses, thus giving the seed maximum amount of light which is needed to produce the ideal sprout: short, dark green and firm.

At Impington Farm, potatoes were not grown in huge quantities; I think the earlies were grown rather as a 'cash crop'. Consequently we did not have an elaborate set-up for the chitting. Instead, a redundant poultry shed on the Poultry Farm was used in which to stack the potato trays. The windows on each side of the shed were not continuous, but had lengths of boarding between them, so the amount of light absorbed into the building was far from ideal. Bearing in mind the 15 cwts of seed needed for each acre, if you grow say 15 acres, the total seed needed is 11 ¼ tons. After distributing this amount into the seed trays at about 2 stones per tray, you need a total of 940 trays, and these take up quite an area in the shed. These were stacked along the length of the shed, about a dozen high, and a maximum of three wide so as not to restrict light to the inner ones more than could be helped.

If the potatoes had been left in the hessian sacks they would have produced unwanted shoots resembling long, thin white tentacles. When allowed to grow like this they are unavoidably damaged when handled, and simply exhaust the energy of the tuber needed to support the early stages in the growth of the plant. Even in the poultry shed, where we'd given them as much care as possible, they still produced a lot of the unwanted long shoots. On wet days Harry would send in Bill Butler and the three regular farm women to take off the extra long shoots, and on a number of occasions I was sent to join them and helped with the de-shooting. We had a long bench at the side of the shed and, starting at one end of the stacks of trays, we would each take a tray to the bench to remove the shoots. These trays would then be re-stacked, leaving a gap between them and the un-treated ones, and gradually working our way along the shed. Whilst removing the shoots, we had to make sure that there were still enough smaller shoots left on the tubers, for a tuber without any shoots would be useless.

Weather permitting, the seed potatoes would be planted round about mid-March. The job was done by hand and could be quite backbreaking and tiring, as I was to find out. The ground had previously been ridged by Edgar, using a double-furrow plough, and we were to plant in the bottom of the ridges. A supply of the full seed trays had been delivered to the field by Curly on his pony lorry. As well as the women and a number of men, there were three or four of us boys for the planting, and Harry came to show the boys what to do. Starting at the end of the field, he arranged the boys, including me, into pairs. Each pair held a tray of seed between them, holding a handle each with one hand. Each boy stood in a furrow and, with the length of the tray they held between them, this left a third furrow between the ones they stood in.

Synchronising their movements as far as possible, the boys were to remove potatoes from the tray with the free hand, and drop them down at just over twelve inches apart, in front of their feet. For a start I was rather frustrated, for the boy with me seemed unable to work together as a team and there was an irritating pulling backwards and forwards on the handles of the tray. In time we got our movements more together, which helped, but the posture felt uncomfortable. The empty furrow left between us as we crossed the field, was planted on the way back. Once the planters had moved a little way across the field and were out of his way, Edgar started to cover up the planted rows, by splitting the ridges over them with his double-furrow plough. I don't remember how long the planting took, but I was certainly pleased when it was finished – it was one job I didn't relish.

Later, about the middle of July, we were able to see the results of our earlier labours. Harry told us that Whitehead's lorry would be coming in the afternoon to pick up a load of early potatoes, so we had to lift some and bag them up for him. Edgar and his horses were again involved, this time with a potato 'spinner'. This machine had a vertical wheel at the back, with a number of long fingers attached which, as the wheel spun round, dug into the soil at the side of a potato row and 'spun' the potatoes out onto the opposite side. These were then picked up into wicker baskets, then transferred into the hessian sacks in which Whitehead's would collect them. When the gang had finished picking up the row of potatoes spun out by Edgar, it was then my job on this particular occasion, to follow him round with a horse and harrow, which brought to the surface the potatoes that had been missed. When these were picked up, Edgar would do a further round with the spinner. A couple of men with a set of scales were stationed at the edge of the field near the farm roadway, to weigh up the sacks into hundred-weights, ready for collection by the lorry. Such was my experience of the growing of early potatoes. I cannot say what the yields were, as I was never told; I imagine about 8 tons to the acre. Neither can I remember the variety – probably the ubiquitous *Arran Pilot*. I believe that some other early varieties used at the time were *Epicure* and *Duke of York*.

Flying Bombs: the start of a Life-long Friendship
. The Second World War was still going on at this time, and it was when we were in the middle of harvesting the early potatoes, that the enemy's *V-1 flying bombs* began to drop on London. The destruction caused by these bombs prompted a new evacuation from the capital and nearly one and a half million people had left before the end of July 1944.[3] Amongst these evacuees was a Mrs Ivy Maish from Annerly, and her two schoolboy sons, Derek and David, who came to stay with a relative in Brampton Road, Cambridge. Derek, who was fifteen – one year younger than me – went to the Labour Exchange to enquire about a temporary job and was directed to Chivers. This was how I got to know him, when he came to work for a while at Impington Farm. When the onslaught of the flying bombs came to an end, they were replaced by the even more destructive *V-2 Rockets*. This continued until February and March of the following year. Quite how long the Maish family stayed in Cambridge I do not know. However, Derek and I

---

[3] *See 'ENGLISH HISTORY 1914-1945' by A.J.P. Taylor (Book Club Associates 1979)*

continued to keep in touch. Later when he and I were both married and with children, both families became firm friends, and this has continued to the present day – a personal result of the wartime flying bombs.

Miscellaneous Tasks
In the same month of July during which the potatoes were lifted, I remember, we were busy with a number of different jobs. Early in the month I spent a number of days with Bill Butler and his three women tying up plum trees, i.e. tying up the branches to prevent them breaking under the weight of the developing plums. Curly had delivered a quantity of long wooden poles to the plum orchards of such varieties as the *Victorias* and *Czars* etc. At each tree, we would count the number of branches, then attach the same number of long lengths of string to one end of a pole. The pole would then be erected up the middle of the tree and, with strips of sacking wrapped to protect the tree, the pole would be supported by tying it tightly to the trunk. The hanging strings were then each extended outwards and tied to the individual branches round the tree; the result looked rather like a maypole.

In addition to the potatoes that were collected by the wholesaler's lorry, other produce was also collected during the same month. I spent a number of days with a gang cutting cabbages. The cut cabbages were put into hessian sacks, about 10 to a sack, and the sacks tied up at the top. As with the potatoes, Whitehead's lorry would arrive during late afternoon, and usually I would help to load him up with the cabbages. It was a similar situation a little later in the month with plums, when the *Early Rivers* were being picked. The plums were weighed up into chip baskets and, at the end of the day the lorry would arrive to collect about 500 of the 12 lb baskets. Strawberries also were being picked now; some of these too were collected by Whitehead, though I think that quite a lot were carted into the jam factory by the farm transport.

****

An (unexpected) Mechanistic Interlude (October '44 – June '45)
My work at Chivers continued pleasantly and interestingly throughout
the summer, sometimes with the horses, at other times with other jobs.
All in all I was very happy there. However, Mum, for some reason had
it in her head that the job was not good for me. For the past two or
three years I had been subject, in the winters, to heavy head colds and I
had had one such cold early in the year while leading for Old George,
though I had not let it bother me too much. In about the September, as
autumn was approaching, Mum began to hint that, before the winter set
in, I ought to think about changing my job. I didn't take much notice of
these hints, and rather than argue, I quietly ignored them. Now,
whether because I had not verbally stated any objections Mum thought
that I agreed with her, I don't know. However, before the end of the
month she told me that she had enquired locally about a job and she had
arranged for us both to call to see the gentleman concerned.

This news was rather a 'bomb-shell' and I didn't know what to do. The
matter couldn't be discussed with Dad for he was away, unfortunately
having been admitted to hospital again for another long course of
treatment. Mum continued her persuasions, and eventually I agreed to
the interview. The prospective job site was only two streets away from
our house in Eden Street. It was a small complex, in Fair Street,
containing a cycle cum motor parts shop and small garage, with a
cycle-repair workshop at the rear. The business name was *'Vic Davis'*
and it was the proprietor himself, Mr. Vic Davis that we were to see. I
called with Mum to see him and it was soon clear to me that the matter
had previously been discussed in some detail and that my employment
there was virtually agreed - a fait accompli. I think that I was in a bit of
a daze at the suddenness with which the situation had come upon me,
but with the continued persuasion, I agreed to the job. My main duties
would be the repair of cycles, in the rear workshop of the
establishment.

Having agreed to take the job, I then had to give in my notice at
Chivers, of course, and I did not look forward to that. With some
embarrassment I handed in a week's notice to Harry. I think that he
was quite surprised to hear that I was leaving, knowing as I'm sure he

did that I had been happy at Chivers. He asked me what I was going to do and I told him that I was to learn to repair bicycles; he put me at ease with a comment that being able to carry out bike repairs would be a useful skill. Well, I worked out my week's notice with mixed feelings. On the one hand I would be sorry to leave Chivers – especially the horses – on the other hand, and trying to make the most of things, I told myself that a job only five minutes walk from home could have its advantages. At the end of the week I put on a brave face, but was sorry to say farewell, for what I thought was the last time, to Impington Farm and the mates I had got to know there.   In the meantime Mum, realising that I would need some overalls, had purchased for me a couple of boiler suits.   On trying one of these on, I thought that I 'looked the part' and, wearing them the following week, I started the new job with a fresh 'image'.

Mr. Davis was a big man with a forceful personality. He led me through a wide gap in the rear of the garage wall, into the cycle workshop. He explained that he would be giving me various jobs from time to time, but the main part of my work would be to repair bicycles. I was shown round the workshop and I noted the details as follows. Along the inner wall was a long bench, which in addition to a number of tools strewn along it, contained a couple of vices of different sizes, plus another gadget which I was told was for adjusting cycle wheels which were out of true. This last mentioned item was made up of an inverted pair of bicycle front forks mounted on a metal frame. Fixed higher up on the wall, in the far corner at the end of the bench, was a large metal cylinder containing compressed air. I was later to learn that the pressurised air was not only used for pumping up car and bicycle tyres, but was also useful for blowing accumulated dirt from all sorts of items.

Along the middle of one end of the workshop were two pieces of equipment for supporting bikes while they were being repaired. One of these was extremely simple: two bicycle chains had been hung down from the ceiling, about 30 inches apart, and at the bottom end of each had been fixed a double hook made out of very thick wire. One set of these was hooked under the cycle handle-bars and the other set under the saddle, to support the bike a few inches off the floor. The second support was a more sophisticated piece of equipment. It was a tubular metal structure, with a circular base that was bolted to the floor, and higher up it had a clamp which supported the bike. You had to lift the bike and place the upright part of the frame – the part beneath the saddle – into the shaped clamp, and then support the bike with one hand while you tightened up the clamp with the other. In spite of its more 'state-of-the-art' appearance, this piece of equipment was not as easy to place the bike in, when you were on your own, as the one with the simple wire hooks.

Against the back wall of the workshop, at a little distance from the cycle supports, was a little round coke-burning 'tortoise' stove' used for giving a little heat in the winter. In the garage, against the dividing wall between it and the workshop, was a large metal sink. This had a tap at the top, which was activated by a foot pump on the floor at the front. This pump circulated, not water, but paraffin oil, which when it was let out of the sink returned into a container in the apparatus for re-circulating. This sink was mainly used for cleaning dirty car parts, but was useful for cleaning all kinds of dirty, oily and greasy items. It was the practice sometimes to use it in conjunction with the air blower, but as I was to find out, this had to done carefully otherwise you could receive a dirty splattering in the face!

All in all I think that I was fairly impressed with the set-up in the workshop, but one thing that did not impress me favourably at all was when I learned what my wages were to be. It seemed that Mr, Davis had persuaded Mum that the job was the equivalent of an apprenticeship during which, as he would be teaching me, I must expect a low wage to begin with. This 'low wage' turned out to be about one-third of the amount that I had earned at Chivers and I complained bitterly to Mum and asked why she had agreed to it. She said something about 'better prospects' but I was not impressed and continued to complain, until at last she agreed that she would try to find out whether there were any official regulations about pay. Who she contacted I never did know, but she seemed to have been able to get someone to intervene with Mr. Davis, without involving herself. The results of this were both satisfactory and rather comical. Instead of admitting that my wages were too low, in order to 'save face' Mr. Davis told me that as I was doing well, he was increasing my pay. He then gave me increments of about two shillings a week, over a number of weeks, until it reached the required amount. Knowing the background, Mum and I both considered that this was rather funny.

I settled down and was not too unhappy with the work. It was a change to be so close to work; it took me less than five minutes to walk from Eden Street round to the garage in Fair Street and, I suppose, I made the most of my new image in my mechanic's overalls. The cycle repair trade in Cambridge, I was soon to find out, was quite a busy one. The numerous undergraduates virtually all used bicycles for dashing around town and many of them did not appear to treat their transport with much care. They never gave a thought to keeping the moving parts oiled; the chains would dry out and stretch until they were far too long, and then give trouble by continually coming off the sprockets. Cotter pins, wheel and pedal cones would come loose without any attempt to adjust them, until the bike got to the stage of being almost unusable. Various accidents would occur, such as riding into walls or high curbs and buckling the front wheels; or falling off and bending one of the pedal cranks, making the pedals inoperative because the bent one fouled the cycle frame.

This last mentioned item, the bending of a pedal crank, was a very frequent happening and Mr. Davis was always happy to have these brought in for repair. This was the only repair job in which he treated the customer dishonestly. Other jobs seemed to be charged on a reasonable basis, related to the time taken, plus the cost of materials used. However, whenever a bike was brought in with a bent pedal crank, you could almost see Mr. Davis mentally rubbing his hands with silent glee. He would look at the damaged crank, then turn to the customer and say: *"Oh dear, you must have come a cropper with that – it really is bent, isn't it. We're rather busy; I'm afraid you will have to leave the bike for a couple of days. To straighten that out I shall have to heat it up and it will cost you seven and sixpence, I'm afraid."*

No sooner had the customer left when Mr. Davis would say to me: "Here, hold this bike for me." Now, he had in the workshop what he called his 'cranking iron'. This was a heavy metal item of about 2 feet 6 inches long, two-thirds of its length being of a round section to act as a handle, the remaining one-third being flat with a couple of notches cut out. He would insert the bent crank inside one of these notches and then, while I held the bike as still as I could, he would place his foot on the end of the bar and use his weight to straighten it out. He would probably have to have one or two more goes at it until he got it looking reasonably straight. An easy seven and sixpence!

It didn't take me very long to learn how to do most of the routine bike repairs that were brought into the workshop. Adjustment of wheel and pedal cones; adjusting the fittings round the steering head of the bike; adjusting the chains – or fitting new chains when needed; adjusting brakes or fitting new brake blocks; replacing rusted or worn-out bearings; mending punctures or fitting new tyres and tubes – all these became second nature after a while. More complicated repairs were those to a 'Sturmey Archer' three-speed hub, or when a wheel rim had become badly out of true. Most of these would be seen to by Mr. Davis himself, though later I did become fairly competent at adjusting the wheel rims. These were dealt with in the gadget with the upturned cycle forks on the bench. The rim is adjusted by using a special little spanner to tighten or loosen, as required, the nipples that hold the spokes in the wheel until, hopefully the wheel can be spun round without any wobbles remaining.

Mr. Davis used to garage one car for a lady driver, and one morning when she came to collect it, he got me to serve her with some petrol. We had just one petrol pump that was worked by hand. The handle turned a wheel with cogs round its rim; these cogs intermeshed with others on a perpendicular slide. You turned the handle clockwise until the slide was pushed up as far as it would go, and then rewound the handle to bring the slide down again. It took one wind and one rewind to pump one gallon of petrol. Petrol was rationed at the time and customers were very particular, after the required amount had been pumped, then the pipe on the pump was manipulated so as to extract the last little drop. There was little activity in the garage itself and motor repairs seemed to be a part-time affair. Although he had an assistant in the shop, Mr. Davis seemed to spend much of his time in there himself. Occasionally a vehicle would be brought in and repairs done on a Saturday by Mr. Davis' two sons, who obviously had other jobs during the rest of the week. Both sons would have been well in their thirties, I think. On one Saturday they worked on the re-bore of an engine in a Rover car and I remember one of them explaining to me some of the details.

I continued with the cycle repairs which, as the weeks went by, seemed to increase in volume to the extent that it was becoming very difficult to keep up with them. Mr. Davis decided that he must employ another boy. The lad he took on was about my age but was very skinny – a lad named John. One unforgettable peculiarity of John, in addition to his thinness, was one slightly bent arm that he could not straighten out completely. After a while, when I had got to know him a little better, I tried to discretely enquire about his pay, in case he was being underpaid as I had been at the first. However, John did not want to go into the matter so I didn't pursue it any more. He was a cheerful lad and we got on well together. Mr. Davis came into the workshop quite a bit for the first few days of John's employment, but as I was now becoming competent with the repairs, he came in less and less, and I found myself teaching John all the repairs that I had learned to carry out.

One little habit of John's which at first annoyed me, but which I gradually came to accept, was the way when he had a fresh bike to start work on, he would rush to grab the purpose built support equipment. Eventually I made a habit of automatically using the lowly hooks, for it was perfectly satisfactory working with these, and left the other one for John; I think that somehow he felt that this gave him more status. As I said we two got on well together; however, being two boys we did occasionally have our 'silly' moments of playing about. Each morning about 11.30 am Mr Davis would disappear – I think that he went for a drink somewhere. This was the time, obviously, for any larking about. The favourite thing, when the coke stove was alight, was to place a little more coke on the fire so that there was no flame at the top, then take the oil can and quickly apply five or six long squirts onto the fresh coke. The round metal lid would then be replaced on top and we would stand back and wait. The oil would run down into the red fire below and suddenly there would be a loud 'whoosh' that would almost blow the lid off the top, which highly amused us.

The winter of 1944-45 came and went and I was not unhappy during that time at Vic Davis'. I no longer had to get up early and cycle to Histon for a 7 am start; now I had only a five minute walk and did not start work until 8.30 am. The workshop itself was warm and comfortable to work in and, all in all I had nothing to complain about. However, when the spring came round I began to have vague feelings of dissatisfaction – that something was missing in life. By the beginning of May I was more consciously aware of what the missing element was. I was yearning for what I had lost: Chivers and the open-air life, and especially working with my beloved horses. As these feelings gradually became stronger, so I began to become increasingly unhappy and dissatisfied, and my discontent became obvious to Mum. One day I complained bitterly about the way I felt, and Mum agreed that if I was that unhappy then perhaps I should try to get back at Chivers. I went to see Mr. Chambers at Impington Farm and explained the situation and, fortunately for me, he was happy to have me back. By the beginning of June '45 I was back where I felt I belonged.

****

Back on the Farm
It was a big relief to have resolved my employment problems and I was very happy to be back on the farm once more. Harry seemed to make a point of asking me all about what I had been doing while at Vic Davis' so I told him that I learned to be competent to deal with virtually all the routine cycle repairs. He commented that this could be a very useful skill and that he could very well make use of it himself. Thinking about this, I realised that I had always noticed how careless I had thought Harry to be with his bicycle. He used it to get about all over the farm and sometimes would ride it over the roughest of ground, where I

65

would never think of riding my bike, and he was always getting his tyres punctured. Whenever he went to see how any of the men were getting on, a gang of men hoeing for instance, he would dash up to the edge of the field, jump off his bike and literally throw it onto the ground in his hurry to get across to the men. Much of the time while riding, he would be standing up on the pedals – the saddle often being stuck at a funny angle and impossible to sit on. I could well understand how Harry would be able to make use of my services, and so it turned out to be. I came to be regarded as cycle-mechanic-in-chief with special responsibility for the maintenance of the foreman's transport.

On the Roof; then Bullied by Turkeys

One of the first jobs I was given after my return to the farm was to assist Charlie Preston, the farm maintenance man. At Park Farm was a large cattle shed that Charlie was working on. The walls of the shed were solid for about half their height, with the top half constructed of 'Yorkshire Boarding' I think it was called. This boarding was fixed vertically to the sides of the building, but with gaps between the boards of about 2 inches. This arrangement protected the cattle from the elements, but let light and plenty of fresh air in. Some of the boards were broken and these Charlie was replacing. His main task however was to repair the roof, which was made of corrugated iron sheets, many of which had rusted and developed holes. It was a case of having to inspect these sheets to find the damaged ones, then to replace them with new ones. This involved a lot of clambering about, as the roof area was huge.

The overlapping sheets were fixed on to the roof framing by means of 'spring-headed' nails – special nails that were knocked through the sheets along the top convex ridges. Each nail had a large domed head that, when knocked down, provided a close watertight covering all round the nail hole in the sheet. When we found a damaged sheet, all these nails had to be taken out again, before the sheet itself could be removed. Charlie did this by means of his 'wrecker bar'. This was a metal bar of about 2 feet in length that had a curled end with a claw at the tip, similar to that on a claw hammer. The claw had to be knocked into position beneath the head of the nail then, using the bent neck of the bas as a fulcrum, the nail could be levered out.

When all the nails had been removed from a damaged sheet it then had to be removed by pulling it from beneath its overlapping neighbour along one side, and the one at its top end. This was where I came in: when Charlie had removed all the nails I would help him to pull the sheet out. Then while he started on the next one to come off, I would take it to the lower edge of the roof and slide it and drop it down onto the ground below. At the end of each day these dismantled sheets would be tidied up into neat piles ready for collection and disposal.

My first day with Charlie was a nice bright sunny one. At breakfast time we climbed down from the roof to get our dockey bags and decided that we would sit in the sun in the yard. We made up comfortable cushions with a couple of folded sacks and sat down with our backs to a fence. We were half-way into our breakfast when suddenly from round a corner came six or seven turkeys. Now, ever since I was a young boy, when I had been painfully pecked on the end of my finger by a cockerel, while pushing chickweed through a wire netting fence for some friends' chickens, I had never liked any kind of poultry. In fact it had given me a phobia about them. I had not seen turkeys in the flesh before – and I thought that they were the most ugly birds I had ever seen.

We carried on with our breakfast, with me keeping a wary eye on the turkeys. At first they didn't take much notice of us, until Charlie decided to throw them a piece of bread. That did it! They fought over the lump of bread, then dashed towards us for more. Charlie shooed them off with a wave of his hand – and they congregated round me. Sitting low down on the ground, besieged by a posse of these big birds I was horrified. The more I tried to disperse them the more persistent they became, dashing up and almost snatching the food from my hand, and I became extremely unhappy. I tried not to show my fear to Charlie, but told him I was fed up with the turkeys and that I was going to move into the shed. I closed my dockey box, picked up my bag and went into a nearby shed to finish my breakfast, pleased to be free of the ugly, troublesome birds.

I spent only a couple of days with Charlie helping to repair the big cattle shed roof. On the second afternoon, Harry came to see how we were getting on. Before he left again he told Charlie that he was going to have to take me away the next day, but that he would send someone else to assist him. Then, turning to me he said that he wanted me to report next morning to Mr. ------ [4] at the Poultry Farm, as Benito, the present young assistant there was leaving in a week's time for a month's leave, and he wanted me to take his place. Irony of ironies!! With my phobia about poultry, and the previous day's encounter with the turkeys, this was the last thing I wanted to hear. However, I said nothing to Harry about my concerns and said that I would go to the Poultry Farm next morning. Rather than confess my dislike of poultry I would have to try to overcome my aversion. That night I found it difficult to dismiss the matter from my mind; I felt that I had the prospect before me of four or five weeks of 'Poultry Purgatory'. Anyway, I had decided that I would make the best of it and get used to the situation.

The Arbury Poultry Farm
I reported at the farm next morning and was taken to find Benito, who was in a loose-box grooming a fat black pony. Benito had a rubber tyred lorry, similar to those on Impington Farm but kept specifically for use on the Poultry Farm. The lorry was drawn by the fat, black pony, whose name was 'Molly'. I was to find out why the pony was so fat. Benito did not get his pony feed from the head horse-keeper at Impington Farm, but was responsible for collecting the pony's feed himself, from the mill at Fieldstead Farm. This feed was kept in metal bins in a feed / harness shed next door to the loose-box. In addition to the usual crushed oats, it seemed that Benito had wangled a supply of kibbled beans as well. He was in the process of feeding the pony when I was introduced to him, and bearing in mind the rations given to the Percherons, I was surprised at the generous amounts he was putting in

---

[4] *Name now forgotten*

68

the pony's manger. Apart from being overweight, the pony appeared to be in very good condition with a fine glossy coat, which Benito took great pains to groom. It was obvious he was fond of the pony by the way he spoke to her.

Before relating any more of my experiences on the poultry farm, perhaps I should describe the farm itself. The entrance to the farmstead was near the western end of Arbury Road, on the north side of the road. The land extended from the farmstead westwards until it abutted the Cambridge-Histon road, then ran northwards until it abutted Cawcutts Farm. This area was occupied by fruit orchards, and through these orchards were farm roadways connecting the two farms, Poultry and Cawcutts.
Another access to the orchards was provided by a gateway on the Cambridge-Histon road, directly opposite the Impington Farm entrance. Just how many acres the orchards occupied I don't know; they had a number of poultry houses scattered amongst them and the outdoor chickens used to roam beneath the trees. Towards Cawcutts Farm the orchards consisted of apple trees, I think, but the nearer ones round the poultry farm buildings were mainly Victoria plum trees.

As well as the top fruit orchards, there was an area with long rows of blackberries, supported by wires on posts. A rather amusing incident occurred one summer in connection with these blackberries, but I will leave its description until the right period. On the farmstead itself, there were a number of large wooden poultry houses, with sun verandas and outside runs, and a farm roadway running through the farm for access. One or two of these sheds, I found, were used for the breeding and rearing of meat rabbits. A large brick building housed the incubator room and an office. The foreman's house was located on the right hand side just inside the Arbury Road entrance. On the left, inside the entrance, a long corrugated iron shed had been converted into living quarters for prisoners of war. It had been divided into sleeping quarters at one end, and a large living area with a large solid-fuel stove in the middle, at the other end. I think that the prisoners who lived in this building were Italians, though I'm not one hundred per cent sure of this, as we also had some German P.O.Ws at one time. There were various other buildings on the farm, including the pony's loose-box and a shelter for the pony-lorry. In addition to Benito and the foreman the staff included one other man and one woman. The Poultry Farm foreman was completely responsible for the livestock operation on the farm. However, the surrounding orchards, in which some of the poultry ran, and the pruning work on the trees, was under the control of Harry Chambers, the general foreman in charge of the local farms.

Benito was of a slightly swarthy complexion and had black hair; his slight accent told me that he was not of British extraction. I later learned that his parentage was half Italian, half Spanish. He turned out to be of a rather excitable temperament, rather a dare-devil and quite a 'character'. When he had finished grooming Molly the pony we took her outside and yoked her up in the lorry. Benito had had orders to transport some crates of chickens to the railway station in Histon. However, we first had to catch and crate them up he told me. "Now for it!" I thought – not looking forward at all to the proposed activity. Firstly Benito took the pony and lorry round to an open-fronted shed that contained stacks of wooden poultry crates. He asked me to back the lorry alongside the shed, while he sorted out some decent crates, so I held Molly's rein and started to back her. Suddenly, as I happened to glance sideways at Benito in the shed, I felt a pain in my left shoulder. What Benito had failed to tell me was that Molly disliked backing. My attention had only been diverted away from the pony for a split second, but during that time she had stuck her neck forward and clamped her teeth right round the deltoid muscle of my shoulder and bitten hard. Luckily being early in the day and still cool, I was still wearing my jacket which gave a little protection, otherwise the damage could have been a lot worse. The pain continued all day, and it took three or four weeks for the shoulder to recover completely.

With the required number of crates transferred onto the lorry, next, it was a case of catching the chickens. These had already been confined in a fairly restricted space at one end of a poultry house, to make it easier to catch them. We drew the lorry round to the shed and took one of the crates inside. Benito was soon catching chickens and stuffing them into the crates, while I went through the motions of trying to catch

70

them myself. While Benito was catching them left, right and centre, I didn't catch one! Psychologically of course I *didn't want* to catch them. In order to cover my lack of ability I complained strongly about the pain in my shoulder – it really was hurting badly – left the catching to Benito and simply lifted the small lid in the crate for him each time he was ready to insert more birds. Making use of the pain in my shoulder as excuse, I managed not to touch any birds on that occasion, but the excuse couldn't go on forever of course. Later, after Benito had gone on leave, I found myself assisting the foreman himself, when such jobs needed doing. As well as filling crates we sometimes had to unload crates, which involved inserting an arm into the crate to grab the chickens. Fortunately, forcing myself to do the work, gradually enabled me to reduce my phobia. This did not go completely as I still do not enjoy handling poultry, but it reduced enough for me to cope with my spell at the poultry farm.

I think that each of the crates held about twelve birds. When the required number had been crated up, Benito tied some prepared labels on to the crates and we delivered them to the station. When we arrived back at the farm it was almost breakfast time, so Benito slipped the pony out of the shafts of the lorry and, leaving her harness on, put her in the loose-box. Here I am sure, she managed to stuff a little more of the feed left over from earlier. As one of the Impington Farm horseman said to me later when he saw me driving her – after Benito had left for his leave – Molly was being killed by kindness. Anyway, we were both ready for our breakfast on this particular morning, and made our way to the incubator room where, as Benito had informed me, it was the custom for the staff to assemble – except the foreman, who would return to his cottage for breakfast.

The incubator room had its own distinctive smell. It contained a number of wooden cabinets with their tops at about table height and which were electrically heated. I seem to remember that they all had glass lids. The other two members of staff, a man and a woman were there and we all four sat in a more open space in the corner of the room. The man, I think, amongst his various duties was in charge of the incubators. His breakfast, I noticed, was comprised of very thin, crispy toast and, after a few days, I observed that this breakfast item did not vary from day to day. He explained that he had had to undergo an operation to remove part of his intestine, and had to be careful with his diet. The lady member of staff, I learned, as well as feeding poultry in the orchards, was responsible for the recording of some 'trap-nested' hens. These hens, I think were housed separately and their nests, in which they laid their eggs, were constructed so that when the hen entered the nest a flap dropped down behind her so that she could not exit the nest again until released by the staff. These birds had numbered rings attached to their legs, allowing their egg-laying capacity to be recorded. I assume that the eggs from the best layers would be the ones used in the incubators for breeding with.

After breakfast, as the foreman had nothing for Benito to do immediately, he suggested that as he was getting low on pony feed that he go and fetch some from the mill. We collected the pony from her loose-box and put her back in the lorry. The seat on Benito's lorry was quite a wide one with room to seat two people, so I sat next to him as we started off. I had assumed that we would go to Fieldstead Farm, where the mill was located, via the main road. However, instead of leaving the farm by Arbury Road, Benito turned the other way and headed towards the orchards. He had decided to keep to the farm roadways and go via Cawcutts Farm, before turning out onto the public road nearer Histon. Now, I had previously heard Benito described as 'hot-headed' or 'reckless', by some of the men, but as I had not before had much contact with him, I was not in a position to judge. However, I was about to be given a demonstration of Benito's proneness to rather madcap actions.

Once we were away from the buildings and out in the orchards Benito flicked the reins on Molly's back and started her off into a smart trot. Now the pony was – shall we say – both metaphorically and literally *full of beans*, and, with her surfeit of the dietary article, she was also it seemed full of wind. As she started into her trot she suddenly emitted a series of noisy and smelly blasts from her rear end, which of course, was unpleasantly just beneath and in front of us. Benito flicked the reins once more, making the pony go faster. The farm roadway was reasonably level, though not as smooth as the public road, and the empty trolley rattled and bounced a bit with the pace. Then, without warning, Benito handed me the reins, got down off the seat and climbed forwards on the shafts. He twisted round and sat on the pony's back, facing backwards, and then smacked the pony smartly on her hindquarters to make her gallop. We galloped along in our madcap progress almost to Cawcutts when, thinking that if we were seen and reported we could be in trouble, I thought it time to slow Molly down before we reached the farm. I was somewhat hindered in this by the fact that Benito, astride the pony, was sitting on the reins, but with a strong pull beneath him I gradually managed to reduce her pace to a sedate walk.

Benito got back on the seat and I handed over the reins to him. We walked the pony through the farmyard and then trotted to the public road where we turned right towards Histon. Once we were over the railway crossing we took the road towards Impington, then further on turned right off this and eventually came to Fieldstead Farm. The person we found there was a girl of about nineteen; I think she may have been one of the Government recruited wartime '*land-girls*' as I seem to remember that she wore the shaped breeches of the land-girl uniform. Benito told her that he wanted some pony feed and from one of the buildings she brought him out a bag of crushed oats, and made out a ticket for it. He asked her for more beans, which she didn't seem very inclined to let him have, but he worked his charm on her and we came away with a further supply. Benito handed me the reins to drive back and I kept to the public road all the way, thus avoiding any more of Benito's zany activities. Back at the Poultry Farm, we unloaded the feed and tipped it into the feed bins, and then Benito went off to find the foreman to see what he had to do next.

On his return he told me that the next job was to kill some cockerels, a job that in my then state of mind, sounded a most unpleasant task. How *extremely* unpleasant it was going to be I could not have imagined, but was about to find out! I am, to this day, still not sure that the operation was intended to be carried out as Benito performed it – or whether it was just one more of his crazy peculiarities. The cockerels had already been put in a crate and were ready for him outside one of the sheds. Next to the crate was a contraption containing about half a dozen cone-shaped objects, about the same size and shape as the cones used by road-men when coning off a section of road, but without the supporting piece at the base. The cones, made of galvanised sheet metal, were open at both ends and suspended in a circle on a metal ring, which was supported on a metal framework. The bigger ends of the cones faced upwards and the lower smaller ends downwards, and the whole thing was designed so that the cones could be spun round in a horizontal circle.

When Benito took one of the birds from the crate, I was expecting him to do – what I had occasionally seen my Grandfather do – break the bird's neck, to kill it. Instead, he stuffed the bird tightly, head first into one of the cones so that its feet were at the top, and its head hanging through the hole at the bottom. He carried on placing the birds in the cones in this fashion until all six were full then, without more ado he held the head of each bird in turn, and slit its throat with the long, thin, blade of a knife. With the blood running and the poor birds twisting their necks in agony, I could barely manage to look. And the final straw was when Benito spun the cones round and the dripping blood spun outwards with the centrifugal force of the motion – it all seemed far too sadistic. I never did enquire any further about the matter – I was just pleased that I never saw it done again, and that I was never called upon to do it. Thinking about it later, I concluded that the real purpose of the cones was to simply bleed the birds *after* they had been killed.

I continued helping Benito and learning more about some of the jobs he carried out, until the end of the week when he left for his four weeks leave. My shoulder, where Molly had bitten me, was still fairly sore and was to take another three or four weeks before the pain had completely gone. During the following month while Benito was away, whenever there was a job needing two people, I had the company of the foreman. With perseverance and the '*gritting of teeth*' I gradually got more used to handling the poultry and reducing my phobia, and so managed to cope with the rest of the period. However, I was very glad when at last Benito returned to work, and I was able to revert to normal.

Pleased to be back on Impington Farm

On reflection I think that my short spell with the poultry was a useful experience. It had enabled me to learn to handle them and to partially overcome my earlier distaste for them – though I still did not *like* them. I was glad to leave behind all the 'beaks and feathers' and get back to dealing with more sensible animals. You could feel close to a horse, which you couldn't with a chicken! Well, there was plenty of work going on back on Impington Farm and everyone was kept pretty busy. Many of the usual gang of local fruit-pickers were with us; they had started on the strawberries in early June, and then the Careless gooseberries. The strawberries were still being picked in July, also the Whinham gooseberries; then about the 20th of the month the Early Rivers plums were becoming ripe for picking.

I was occupied with all the usual summer tasks: tying and supporting the plum tree branches; cabbage cutting and bagging; then the harrowing out of the early potatoes after the first 'picking up' behind the potato 'spinner'. Some of the picked fruit would be destined for use in the Chivers factory, some to be put on rail at the local station for elsewhere, and I was sometimes involved in carting it. The fruit for sending away on rail would have to be weighed up in boxes or baskets before leaving, and this weighing would be done on the headland at the orchard. And this too was a job I was asked to do.

Bill Butler was the man put in charge of the orchards and the fruit-picking gang. His three regular farm women Doris, Rene and Olly, joined the other pickers and spent the season picking fruit. Virtually the whole of the various fruit crops were picked on a *'piece-work'* basis – in other words, the more you picked the more you earned. As I was to find out later, Doris, Rene and Olly were by far the champion pickers; no-one else could keep up with their speed of picking and they were able to earn quite a bit of money during the fruit season. Bill himself organised the work of all the fruit-picking gang and moved their ladders for them from tree to tree. Many of the trees were quite tall and consequently long ladders were needed to reach the fruit. These ladders were of heavy timber construction and had metal spikes attached at the bottom which, when the ladder was placed against the tree, would be thrust into the ground to prevent the ladder from twisting. Care would also be taken to rest the top of the ladder against a suitably strong branch.

Bill was an expert at ladder moving. The ladders were long and heavy and for one person to lift one from the horizontal, to the upright position, was no mean feat. Once the ladder was in position against a tree, it was not lowered each time it was moved to another tree, but was kept upright. Bill had the required technique down to a fine art: he would lift the ladder to remove the spikes from the ground, then turn it and place one of the side '*stiles*' against his shoulder. He would grip one of the lower rungs with both hands and lift the ladder just clear of the ground. Then, with the ladder tipped back ever so slightly so as to rest against his shoulder – but still almost perpendicular – carefully walk out from between the branches with the balanced ladder and place it either further round the tree, or take it to another tree, as required. When walking with the balanced ladder, care had to be taken to walk *between* the branches of the trees, for if you caught a high branch against the ladder it could be knocked out of your control.

As previously mentioned, Mr. Chambers was very careless with his bike. He was frequently getting his tyres punctured, often unnecessarily I think, had he been slightly more careful where he rode. In consequence I was often called on to go back to the farm to repair the bike for him. Sometimes I would find that a thorny patch of ground that he had ridden over had caused four or five punctures in the same wheel. When I had returned to the farm after my cycle-repairing period at Vic Davis', Harry had very soon got to rely on me for keeping his bike in good repair. In addition to the puncture repair equipment he already had, I had persuaded him to get me a set of cycle spanners. These I kept hidden inside the tool loft so I knew where to find them when they were needed and usually, whenever I mended punctures I would look round the bike to see what else needed doing, and carry out whatever was needed. One of the parts that Harry was very hard on was the chain that drove the back wheel. At times he used to ride over such rough ground that he had to '*stand*' on the pedals in order to keep going, and the strain of this kind of treatment soon stretched the chain, and I often had to tighten it up for him. At one point it got to such a bad state that I told him that I couldn't do any more to it, so he sent me to a shop in the village to buy a new chain, which I then fitted for him.

In the September of 1945, we had to deliver a consignment of Worcester apples to the railway station, destined I would imagine, for one of the London markets. I took one of the pony lorries to the orchard, where the apples had been weighed up into wooden boxes, collected a load of these and went off happily to the station. On arrival at the station goods yard I found out which was the box-wagon that was to be used for the apples and then drew the lorry alongside the open door of the wagon. I had successfully transferred most of the load when suddenly, with a box of apples in my hands I tripped while stepping across from lorry to wagon. I had evidently been rather careless when I had drawn the lorry alongside the wagon and had not placed it close enough for safety. In an instant I found myself falling between the two vehicles, still holding the box of apples. As I went down I landed heavily with my back against the metal edge of the trolley and felt a sharp pain from the initial knock, and then the graze as I continued down. Recovering slightly from the shock, I managed to pass the box of apples onto the floor of the wagon, and then slowly to wriggle up and out of my predicament.

A moment later Harry appeared on his bike. He had seen the whole thing happen as he had turned into the station yard and he rushed up, quite concerned as to the damage I might have sustained. He tried to persuade me to go to the nearby factory to see the nurse there; however, still in shock I suppose, I declined to go. Instead I decided that I could manage to take the pony back to the farm, and then as I did not feel too good, I would go home. As Harry's continued urging failed to persuade me to do as he said, he loaded the remaining few boxes of apples and let me go back to the farm with the pony. I managed to un-harness her and return her to her loose-box, then, in great discomfort, to cycle home. Luckily I had not broken any bones and, after a week off, was feeling much better. During the week I had a visit from Claud Archer, sent by Harry, to bring me some cash. I remember him showing me a piece of paper and asking me to sign for the money. In my naivety I didn't read the paper before signing it, but on looking back I assume that the payment was in compensation for my accident and I was probably signing my agreement that it was in *full and final settlement*. How much the payment was I cannot now remember.

With the resilience of youth, after about a week or ten days my back had virtually recovered and I went back to work. I spent a few enjoyable weeks working with the horses, but one day in the October Harry told me that when the pruning started shortly, he would want me to team up with Herbert Hankin for the winter and 'Herbie' would teach me how to prune. My first reaction to this, though I didn't say anything, was a feeling of disappointment. I had noticed the Pruners at work during the winter time and, to a lad used to moving around with the horses, their less strenuous occupation appeared to me to be somewhat dull – a job for old men. No, I wasn't impressed with the prospect – and I certainly didn't relish the thought of losing my involvement with the horses. However, I thought that I had better comply with what Harry wanted me to do; to learn a bit about pruning would be a useful experience, anyway.

Stack Thatching
The thatching of corn stacks was always carried out on Impington Farm, by Charlie Camps, and his mate Ken Fishpool. Charlie was the experienced thatcher; Ken used to assist him by preparing the straw. I was able to watch this operation for a while, when on one occasion I was asked to deliver the straw to be used. On my arrival at the stacks Charlie and Ken were already there and had set up Charlie's long thatching ladder against the stack, about 3 feet from one end of the stack. The ladder was positioned at such an angle that the top portion rested flat on the sloping roof of the stack, reaching all the way to the top. Charlie told me where he wanted the straw unloaded, a short distance away from the side of the stack, then, as I started to unload it he buckled on a pair of pads which covered his knees, and Ken wound some sacking round his lower legs and tied it on. Other equipment previously delivered to the site were bundles of split hazel sticks, each about 2 feet long and pointed at one end, a wooden mallet, a short-

handled rake, some balls of string, a small open-topped metal tank filled with water, and a bucket.

When I had unloaded a good-sized heap of straw, Charlie climbed up onto his ladder and immediately the purpose of the knee-pads became clear, as I saw him rest his knees against the rungs of the ladder. He was obviously going to be up that ladder for some considerable time and his knees would certainly need the protection afforded by the pads. Meanwhile Ken had begun shaking out with a fork some of the straw into a separate smaller heap, and then dampening it thoroughly with water from the tank. After this, using his hands, he began pulling out the straw in front of his legs into substantial, long tight bundles, or *'yelms'* as I believe the correct term is, making them compact and tight with pressure against his legs. Here the purpose of the sacking he had tied on was clear – it protected his legs from the dampness of the straw.

As each yelm was ready Ken would take it up the ladder to Charlie who, starting at the bottom corner of the stack, would lay it length-wise *up* the stack, with each succeeding higher yelm overlapping the one beneath it in a similar fashion to overlapping house tiles. When the first space between the edge of the stack and the ladder had been covered in this way, Charlie would hold a piece of wood across each layer of the yelms to keep them in place, then give them a light raking to ensure that any out-of-place tufts of straw were directed downwards. After this, the hazel sticks would be hammered into the roof on each side of the covered layer, and string tied across each succeeding layer of yelms to hold them in place. Charlie would then have to descend briefly from the ladder to move it across, ready to deal with the next adjoining section of roof. When both sides of the roof were completely covered, the protruding straw at the ridge and the eaves of the stack would be trimmed with a sheep-shearing tool to make them neat and tidy. The smart-looking stack, with its new *'hat'* was then quite watertight and could safely be left until it was time to thresh it.

Pruning the Blackberries

It didn't seem five minutes since Harry had told me that he would want me to join Herbie Hankin to learn to prune; but now it was the end of October and time to start. Most of the pruning on the farm was carried out by three men: Herbie Hankin, Charlie Camps and Ken Fishpool. Charlie and Ken were regular mates and usually worked together. I believe that Herbie's previous mate had now retired, hence the reason for teaming me up with him, I suppose. I had had a little contact with Herbie, who would be in his fifties, and had found him to be a pleasant man to get on with, so I had no qualms about working with him from this point of view. Ken Fishpool, of about forty years of age, was also an easygoing sort of man. His mate Charlie, in spite of mature years – I would guess he was nearly sixty – was a '*show-off*' and, at the least opportunity would boast about the exploits of his younger days, so much so that you would become completely bored with his stories. Another man who would occasionally help out with the pruning was Charlie Wrycroft, the foreman's assistant.

I had expected that my first introduction to pruning would be in the main fruit orchards to the south-west of the farm, where I had led the horse for Old George. However on my first day with Herbie we went instead to the poultry farm, to deal with some rather neglected rows of blackberries. Each row of blackberries had three thick horizontal wires that were supported on heavy posts, some of the posts being made from round telegraph poles, and others from railway sleepers. The blackberry plants were positioned about 18 feet apart in the rows. The method of growing them, Herbie explained, was to train the canes all in one direction along the wires to fruit in one year, and to tie in the new growth of that year in the opposite direction, to fruit the following year. Thus the direction of the fruiting canes would alternate from year to year, and no disease spores could drop from the older canes onto the young ones. That was the theory; however, owing to pressure of work, the plants had been allowed to fruit on the same canes for two years and new growth had not yet been tied in, so everything was now in rather a jumble.

The blackberries were very thorny, but I was well protected with a pair of thick leather pruning gloves with which Harry had provided me. He had also given me a pair of '*Rolcut*' secateurs, plus a pruning saw of about 18 inches in length. The first job to do with the blackberries was to cut out all the fruited canes, but before this could be done the strings which held them to the wires had to be released. Luckily I had a shut-knife with me that I could use for this. On Herbie's suggestion we stationed ourselves one on each side of a row and gradually worked along it, cutting out the old canes. It was an advantage having one of us each side, for in some places where the new growth got in the way, it was easier to pull out from one side rather than the other. Where the canes were very jumbled we had to cut the older ones into shorter lengths before we could disentangle them and get them out. Once we had done this job along the full length of a row, we would then go back along the row and tie in the new canes ready for fruiting the following summer.

How many days it took us to complete all the rows I cannot now remember, but when we had finished they all looked much tidier and I felt quite proud of a job well done. Furthermore, my earlier impressions of Herbie were correct: he was a pleasant chap to work with and I had no regrets on that score. When we had reached the end of the job, Harry asked us to start pulling out the canes that we had cut off, from between the rows and to burn them on a nearby piece of open ground. Normally this job would have been done by Bill Butler and his three farm women, but it seems that at the time they were busy on a different job elsewhere, from which they could not be spared. I quite enjoyed burning the canes; there is something pleasant about an outdoor fire.

First Introduction to Blackcurrant Growing.
Shortly after our spell on the poultry farm sorting out the blackberries, I arrived at the farm one morning to find that Herbie was off sick. Harry told me that he was sending me to prune some *blackcurrants*, but said to hold on for a few minutes as he was sending a lad named Peter with me and needed to find some secateurs and gloves for him. Peter arrived for work shortly after, and was given the secateurs and gloves,

which Harry had just fetched from his office, plus his instructions as to work. I was a bit surprised that Peter was coming with me as I knew that he normally didn't take any part in the pruning. We were told that we would find Charlie Camps and Ken Fishpool already at the blackcurrants and that they would show us what to do.

Peter and I biked down the fen to the field that Harry had directed us to, and found Charlie and Ken. They were in this particular field for the first time that morning and had just commenced work on two rows of blackcurrants at the left-hand side of the field. I was most surprised to find that they were cutting down the bushes almost to ground level. To me the bushes looked quite well-grown and sturdy, each having an average, I would guess, of seven or eight nice strong straight shoots, of about 2 feet tall. All these shoots were being cut off and it looked like a *'slaughter of the innocents'*! I asked why they were having be to cut down. Ken explained that they were young plants and it was too soon to let them fruit; the cutting down strengthened them for future years.

At that point Charlie took over. "Come on then boys" he said, "get stuck into the next two rows and I'll show you what to do". Now, Charlie was in his element when he had the chance to give orders to youngsters: dictatorial and bombastic. He was completely different to Herbie who, as I had found, was able to impart his knowledge in a perfectly pleasant way. Not so Charlie – he really got your back up and made you seethe inside. He showed us how to cut off the blackcurrant shoots, leaving just two buds intact at the bottom of each shoot. You cut off the shoot just above the higher of the two buds, cutting as far as possible to an outward pointing bud. He also instructed us as to exactly how the cut should be made, near enough so as not to leave a snag above the bud, but not so close so as to damage it. We had a go at it and did two or three bushes each, while Charlie stood and watched us. Satisfied with us at last, it seemed, he went back to his own row and left us to get on with ours.

It didn't take us very long to get used to the job; so long as you were careful with your positioning of the cuts, the job was quite a simple one. After a while Peter got slightly ahead of the rest of us in the rows, and seeing this Charlie barked at him to hold back and to keep in line with us. Peter, who I could see was very unhappy at being shouted at, took no notice; whereupon Charlie marched across to Peter's row to have a close look at his *'cuts'*, obviously hoping to find fault and lend weight to his demand for Peter to hold back. Luckily he could not find anything to criticise, which annoyed him, and he then started shouting again that we were all to keep together. By this time, I too was beginning to find the rather slow, steady pace of the older men a little irksome. Suddenly, and without any warning, Peter said, *"I'm off – I'm going to work on the other side of the field"*. Before Charlie could quite take in this unexpected show of mutiny, Peter was half-way across the field. *"Come back here, you young b...r !"* bawled Charlie. Peter took no notice and kept going.

I was in a bit of a quandary as to what to do. Making the excuse that Harry had sent Peter to work with me, I said that I had better go across and stay with him. Charlie objected, but I ignored him and went to join Peter. He was still seething at the treatment he had received and vowing to teach Charlie a lesson. I agreed with him that Charlie was a *'pain'* to work with, and that it wouldn't do Charlie any harm to see that we didn't intend to put up with his bullying ways. Talking about it, and egging each other on, I suppose, we decided that we would indeed keep up a smart pace with the work, whether Charlie liked it or not. We felt we had the upper hand, for if we did more work than Charlie, he couldn't very well complain to the foreman about that. *"We'll rattle Charlie's cage"* said Peter. About three or four hours later, we had done about half as much work again, as the others.

Later in the day Harry came to see how we were getting on. He called to see Charlie and Ken, before coming across to speak to us. Whether he received any complaints from the others, we didn't know, but although he didn't say anything, we could tell that he was quite pleased with the work we had done. He stood and chatted for a while, telling us that although what we were doing to the young bushes might appear wasteful, it allowed them to build up their energies. Next year they would grow an even bigger bush of young shoots and then, in the year after would produce a large crop of fruit, and would be expected to carry on their productive lives for a further ten years. Before leaving, he told us to expect a visit later in the afternoon from Doug Foster, who would be collecting some of the blackcurrant shoots we had cut off, to use as *'cuttings'* for propagation. He suggested that if we held on to the shoots in our left hands as we cut them, we could drop them along the rows in some useful sized bundles, ready for Doug to pick them up. From then on that is what we did.

Doug Foster arrived about four o'clock on his motor cycle combination. Whether Harry had told him of the instruction that we were to lay the cuttings ready in bundles I don't know, but he didn't stop to see Charlie and Ken, but came straight to us. Doug I think was in charge of the whole of the propagation of new fruit trees and bushes on the Chivers farms. The side-car on his motor cycle, was in the form of a big box with sliding doors at the side for access. It was divided in two horizontally with an internal shelf. He asked us to help him pick up the cuttings we had dropped ready and to take them to the side-car. Then, before loading any in, he sat and cut them up into approximately 10 inch lengths, ready for using as propagation cuttings, and tied them up into bundles. He then stood these bundles upright on both the bottom and the shelf in the side-car, which must have held, I would guess, at least four or five hundred cuttings, or more. Adding the information about using the prunings for propagation, to what Harry had told us, cutting the bushes down no longer seemed wasteful.

Harry had told Peter and me to carry on in the blackcurrants until the field was finished. Charlie and Ken did not come any more; I imagine that they were sent to make a start on the pruning of the *'top fruit'*. We were pruning the blackcurrants for quite a number of days – just how long it took to complete them I cannot now remember. Neither can I recall the name of the variety of the currants. Numerous varieties were grown on the farm and names such as the following come to mind: *Baldwin, Hatton, Mendip and Westwick.* Later on in my pruning experience I learned how to prune some of the established bushes, which of course is a little more complicated than cutting young bushes down. Subsequently the blackcurrant became one of my favourite fruits to grow and, making use of the knowledge gained at Chivers, the bushes in my current garden (in 2008) are still vigorous after 16 years. I was able, too, to develop my own simplified method of growing and harvesting them, which I have written about elsewhere.

The Pruning Equipment

Cutting down the blackcurrant bushes had been a fairly simple job. When I got on to the general pruning work with Herbie things were not quite so simple and there was more to learn. However, before going into that, it would perhaps be a good idea to list the various items of equipment involved in the work. The following list is fairly comprehensive:

Secateurs: these were a brand named 'Rolcut'; they had a single cutting blade which, when a cut was made, came to rest on a relatively soft brass anvil. The Rolcut secateur was a very robust tool and was the one we used most of the time for dealing with gooseberries, currants, and all the established top fruit trees. If the blade was kept sharp, the tool was very good to handle and, bearing in mind the thousands of cuts it was called upon to make it stood up to the job extremely well. It was constructed so that when the parts did get too worn, they could be replaced.

Pruning Knives: these came in various sizes, and also with a choice of different handles, so it was a matter of the individual preferences of the users. The one common factor was the curved blade specially made for pruning, and if this was kept sharp, it could make an extremely clean and precise cut and was valued in particular for use in the training of *young* fruit trees.

Rub Stones: for the sharpening of both knives and secateurs.

Leather Gloves: these were unlined gloves made of very thick leather; I think that they were possibly made of cowhide and they gave complete protection from the thorns on such plants as gooseberries and blackberries. They were also useful when working in frosty weather.

Pruning Saws: these saws had a blade of about 18 – 20 inches long with a single cutting edge and, if the teeth were sharp and well-set, they would cope with virtually any sized branch that had to be dealt with in the orchards.

Ladders & Step-Ladders: various lengths of ladders would be used, depending on the height of the trees being worked on. Some tall, three-legged step ladders were also used and these were often easier to use in the apples and pears than were the ordinary ladders.

'Long-Arm' Pruners: these were constructed of a shaft of timber of about 1½ inch square section, with a metal hook at one end to which was fixed a hinged cutting knife. Attached to this knife, and running down the shaft through screw-in rings was a stout wire, attached to a handle near the bottom of the shaft. The tool was used by hooking the top hook round the shoot to be cut off, then pulling the handle down-wards to operate the knife. These tools could vary in length; the ones we used at Chivers were about 8 - 10 feet long. They were used while standing on the ground and allowed you to reach fairly high up without the use of steps or ladder. The cut they produced was not as neat or precise as those done by knives or secateurs as you couldn't get close enough to see it as clearly, but they were useful where the branches were difficult to get at.

Twivel: I cannot find this word in the dictionary, but it is what we used to call a tool shaped very much like a pick-axe. One end of the steel head was about 4 inches wide with a sharp cutting edge and was mainly used for chopping off the suckers which sometimes grew at the base of fruit like gooseberries or greengages.

'Monkey' Winch: this was a hand operated metal winch for pulling up dead or diseased fruit trees. First the tree branches would be cut off, leaving short protruding stubs at the top of the trunk. The winch would be positioned between this tree and another tree. Then a metal cable from the winch would be affixed round the top of the trunk to be pulled out, just below the branch stubs. This would prevent the cable slipping off the top. A second cable would then be attached round the other tree trunk, just above ground level. A long metal lever above the winch could then be worked backwards and forwards by

one or two men, to start the pull on the tree; each pull on the lever would result in a movement of about a couple of inches on the cable. The continuous working of the lever would eventually pull out the tree, complete with most of its roots, leaving the 'anchor' tree – which would have been padded with sacking – undamaged.

All the above equipment, *with the exception of the pruning knives,* was provided by the firm. The knives were chosen, purchased and owned by the individual men, and they all took pride in keeping them sharp and ready for use.

My Induction into the Practice of Pruning

I had had a little taste of pruning when Herbie and I had worked on the blackberries at the poultry farm, as already related. However, I now felt that having left the horses behind for a while and being paired with Herbie for the winter, I was to start pruning 'proper'. It wasn't long before I was being initiated into the various pruning terms; learning to distinguish between the different parts of the trees – *branches, leaders, laterals, spurs, stubs, water shoots,* and how to tell the difference between *'growth' buds* and *'fruit' buds.* Herbie was a joy to work with; he was always cheerful and easygoing and would explain and demonstrate the work in a straightforward way. For the first week I was with Herbie, we also saw quite a bit of Harry the foreman who would come to check how I was getting on. He would tell me that for any pruning cut you made, you should always be able to give the reason why you did it – which rather made you concentrate hard when he was watching.

Gooseberries

The first bout of pruning that Harry set us, was on the gooseberries. These bushes were, I think, a *'filler'* crop: they had been planted in the rows of an apple orchard, three bushes between every two trees. They made use of the space between the apple trees until the trees grew too big. When the canopy of the apples expanded so as to restrict the light getting to the gooseberry bushes, these would eventually be grubbed up, but in the meantime they would provide a useful crop for quite a number of years. The bushes we worked on were sizeable, well-established bushes, with good strong branches containing plenty of fruit spurs along their lengths. The main requirement of the pruning was to keep the middles open to allow plenty of light and air into the bush, so any new growth that was crossing the middles had to be cut out. A certain amount of young growth would be kept each year, being *spurred back* to produce new fruit spurs. Occasionally we would come across a bush where a branch had been broken off. In this case we would try to replace it by directing the growth of a new shoot into the gap, to replace the missing branch. A further job was to remove any *suckers* growing from the bush, either from its stem, or from below ground. Those above ground could often be *pulled* off, but for the ones below ground the use of the *twivel* was usually required.

Blackcurrants + One of Charlie's Tales

How long it took us to complete the gooseberries, I cannot remember. Meanwhile Charlie and Ken, the other Pruners, were working on fruit elsewhere. Occasionally, where an extra large number of trees or bushes was involved, Harry would put all four of us together on the same area. This meant that neither pair would be stuck for an excessive amount of time on one job before passing on to a different area. This applied to our next job, the blackcurrants, of which we had a huge number of bushes of varying varieties, and so Charlie, Ken, Herbie and I found ourselves all together pruning these bushes. Now, the more folk you have working together, inevitably the more the chattering that goes on – which normally helps to pass the time quite pleasantly. But, as I have remarked earlier, Charlie tended to be a bit of a show-off and he was in the habit of telling what I regarded as *'tall stories'*, which, when you heard them one after the other, could become rather a bore to listen to.

One of Charlie's stories was about the time when he was in the army, in Egypt, during World War 1. His platoon, which was advancing along a wadi was being pinned down, he said, by a solitary sniper who was holed up in a pretty impregnable position and was firing at them from behind some kind of bullet-proof metal screen. Until this sniper was dealt with the platoon was stuck where it was. Well, Charlie volunteered to deal with the situation and said that he knew how to deal with this annoying sniper. After attaching various pieces of leafy camouflage to his person, Charlie crept forward on his own until he got within firing range of the sniper, and himself hid in a hole in the ground so that he could avoid the sniper's fire. His plan, he said, was to produce some *psychological* damage on the sniper. Getting out his watch, he checked the time and then fired his rifle, causing the bullet to produce a loud twang against the sniper's metal screen. Carefully consulting the watch, he continued to fire at the screen every 30 seconds, causing the sniper to become jittery while waiting for the expected clang in front of him. According to Charlie this had the desired effect – eventually the sniper could stand it no longer and came out of his hideout holding a white cloth of surrender, when Charlie promptly took him prisoner and marched him back to the platoon commander. That was one of Charlie's stories – I wasn't sure whether I ought to regard it as a *tall story*!

Herbie would occasionally tell me a few tales about his younger days, though they were never boastful in the way that Charlie's were. One of Herbie's tales was quite amusing and worth telling, but I will save it for later and get back to the blackcurrant pruning. It is the practice to deal with blackcurrants completely differently to the way gooseberries are treated. In order to make these differences clear, let's go back briefly for a little more information on the gooseberry, before going into details about the blackcurrant. The gooseberry, as indicated above, is grown on a leg, or stem, with a number of permanent branches above that bear the gooseberries on fruiting spurs. As long as a little new growth is retained each year, this permanent framework will go on bearing fruit quite happily year after year for a good number of years. The 6 – 8 inch tall stem enables hoeing to be done right up to the bush, making it easier to keep the weeds down. To achieve this clear stem, and to avoid sucker growth as far as possible, all the buds, on the original cutting used for propagation, are removed before insertion in the soil, *except* for those at the top which are needed to produce the branches. To make this a little clearer, imagine a 20 inch gooseberry cutting you are about to propagate. At the top you have left intact the buds from which will grow the permanent branches. Immediately below this is an 8 inch length, with all the buds removed, to leave above ground for the stem. The remaining 8 inch length at the bottom, also dis-budded, goes into the soil to form roots.

Now about the blackcurrants. The main tool used was the Rolcut secateurs; the pruning saw would be needed occasionally when cutting out older branches that were too thick for the secateurs. The important thing to know about blackcurrants is that they bear the bulk, and the best of their fruit on young wood of the previous season's growth. It is important therefore to encourage the growth each year of a continued supply of this young wood, preferably good strong shoots arising directly from ground level, and *not* to let the bushes grow tall on older wood. If the bushes *are* allowed to grow taller, they will bear a certain amount of fruit on short young side shoots produced on the branches, but these will *not* be as productive. Also, the higher the bush becomes, the higher will be the proportion of old wood that develops and the lower will be its fruiting potential. For this reason the standard pruning practice for blackcurrants, is to remove at least one third of the old branches each year so as to direct more of the bush's energy into younger growth. This need for strong young growth is also the reason for the type of cutting used in the blackcurrant's propagation. *All the buds,* including those below ground, are left intact on the cutting; *unlike* the gooseberry where suckers are *not* wanted, the more growth obtainable direct from the ground, the better it is, in the case of the blackcurrant.

This then explains roughly what our pruning of blackcurrants involved. Basically we were cutting out some of the older branches, but also thinning out some of the young shoots at the bottom of the bush. Having been treated like this regularly each year, the bushes would be furnished with plenty of new young shoots arising from the ground. Cutting down some of these achieved two things: it *spaced them out*, so as to give those remaining plenty of light and air. It also produced more shoots for the next season from the couple of buds that we left intact just above ground level when we cut them. Come the picking season, the different varieties would ripen at slightly different times, so there was not a rush to pick them all at the same time. The variety, however, did not affect the way they needed to be pruned – they were all treated in the same way. We had a substantial acreage of blackcurrants to deal with, and would be working on them for a considerable amount of time. When we eventually were able to leave the currants to work on the top fruit, it was a welcome change to be able to stand up to deal with the trees, rather than continually bend down over bushes!

Apples

The next session of pruning for Herbie and me was in one of the apple orchards; Charlie and Ken were sent elsewhere – possibly on some other apples in a different orchard. For this job we each had a tall wooden step-ladder for dealing with the higher branches that could not be reached from the ground. The trees were well-established and of a fair height, but not as tall as they would eventually be when they reached maturity, so we would not be needing long ladders. The previous pruning the trees had received had resulted in an orchard of nicely shaped trees, with open centres and evenly spaced branches, all with access to the maximum amount of light. Our present job therefore had nothing to do with training the basic framework of the trees, which had all been done in earlier years. The need now was to deal with the laterals, or side growths, on each of the branches, plus the *tipping back* of the branch *leaders* to keep the branches growing in the required direction.

Herbie was quite good at showing me what to do, and explaining the reasons for doing it. He pointed out the difference between *growth* buds and *fruit* (or *blossom*) buds; the *growth* buds were smaller and flatter on the stem, whereas the *fruit* buds were fatter and stood out more. Once this had been pointed out I found that it was fairly straightforward to tell the difference. Observing these fruit buds more closely, I noticed that whilst occasionally you saw a single fruit bud on its own, generally they were in groups of anything from two, to about half a dozen buds, on short stems. These 'stems', Herbie told me, were in fact known as *fruit-spurs*. As they grew and extended in length they would develop more buds and they would often branch out to form *spur systems*. On older trees these *spur systems* would sometimes develop

91

so many buds, that this would result in very small fruit, making it necessary to cut back the branching spurs in order to restrict the number of buds they contained.

To get back to the job in hand: we were working on well trained trees of good shape, so our main task now was to encourage the growth of fruit spurs along the lengths of the branches. This was to be done by cutting back the young *lateral* growths to leave five or six buds, with the aim, hopefully, of producing fruit spurs. Herbie explained that some apple varieties responded to this treatment better than others; they, like the trees we were working on, were known as *spur bearers*. Other varieties that didn't respond so well were those known as *tip bearers* and these tended to bear their fruit on the tip ends of the lateral shoots, so it was the practice to thin out these shoots, but not to cut them back. We got into a routine of working on each tree, starting off at opposite sides of the tree and working round it in a clockwise direction completing one branch at a time. When the spurring had been done along a branch, the *leader*, the extension growth at the very top end of the branch, would be cut back by about a third of its length. This cut would be made just beyond a suitable bud, to ensure that branch continued to grow in the right direction.

Working in this organised fashion meant that as we worked our way round the tree, for most of the time we were facing each other, which made conversation easier. Talking of conversation, perhaps now is the time to tell you one of Herbie's stories that I mentioned above. This particular story was about a strange kind of weight-lifting activity that he used to practice in his younger days; his speciality was to lift weights with his teeth. He had a thick leather mouthpiece that had a metal ring to which ropes could be clipped, after they were fastened to the object that was to be lifted. He would practice in private, he said, until he reached the point where he could lift some quite heavy weights off the ground. He would have the equipment to hand in his bicycle basket and, at a suitable time during the dockey break he would steer the conversation round to lifting weights. Then, pointing to some heavy object he said that he would bet anyone a 'tanner' that he could lift it with his teeth.

On looking at the item in question, and judging that Herbie's chance of lifting it was unlikely, one of his work-mates would usually take up the challenge and bet him sixpence that Herbie couldn't do it. Herbie told me that after getting the chaps to manoeuvre the weight so that he could fix up the ropes round it, he would stand over it, put the leather in his mouth and take up the slack in the ropes. Then he would start to tug upwards, grunt and puff quite a bit to make it look extremely difficult. With his incredulous work-mates looking on he would make what seemed like a last-gasp effort, and lift the weight a couple of inches off the ground – to the dismay of the chap who had bet the sixpence. Having seen what had looked like Herbie's maximum lift, someone would challenge him to add even more weight for another lift. By keeping the weight under the amount he knew he was capable of, but making each lift look terribly hard to achieve, Herbie managed to win quite a number of bets before reaching a weight that he had to admit was too much for him. Now, Herbie's teeth when I worked with him were false ones – whether this had anything to do with his earlier weightlifting activities I don't know. He used to smoke a pipe at work, and when he put it in his mouth his dentures, which were rather loose, used to make a resounding 'click' as he clamped the pipe between them; bearing in mind his story, this always used to amuse me.

The *Young* Apple Trees
It took us about two weeks to complete the pruning in the orchard we had been working in, and then Herbie and I were transferred to deal with another plot containing *young* apple trees. These trees were only about three years old and the object of pruning them was to train them into nicely shaped trees with evenly spaced branches. The step-ladders were now no longer needed, as we could reach the trees working from the ground. As Herbie had taught me, winter pruning affected the vigour of a tree: in general the harder the pruning, the more vigorous would be the resulting growth. The leading shoots at the ends of the branches were known as *leaders*. When one of these was cut back it would normally be stimulated to grow at least three shoots from the buds just below the cut. Care must be taken to make the cut just above a bud that points in the required direction, so as to continue the correct

line of the branch outwards from the stem, or trunk. The growth from this end bud would then become the new *leader* of the branch, and the new lower growths the new laterals for bearing the fruit spurs.

The growth on the tree did not, of course, always correspond to the ideal requirements: one of the leaders perhaps had grown much stronger and longer than its neighbours and was making the branches look unbalanced. Bearing in mind that the harder you cut it back, the stronger it would grow, you would therefore prune it more lightly than its neighbours, and in turn cut the neighbouring branches harder back to encourage them to catch up. At the time, this treatment made the tree look even more lopsided, but you had to think ahead and imagine the resulting new growth, and this kind of thing made the pruning of these *young* trees more satisfyingly creative. Another problem could be where you had too wide a space between two branches, again making the tree unbalanced. In this case you could often prune one of the lateral shoots on a neighbouring branch so as to direct a new shoot to grow to fill the gap – thus creating a new branch.

It was one morning during our spell of working on these young trees that we had one of Harry's frequent visits to see how the work was progressing. Whilst he was talking to us, Charlie Wrycroft arrived together with another man we had never seen before. After briefly mentioning that the gentleman in question was 'Professor' Thompson, a horticultural fruit advisor, Harry left us and went across to where Charlie Wrycroft and the 'advisor' were talking, some little distance away from us. We later learned from Harry that Mr. Thompson had been involved in various pruning trials at the Long Ashton Horticultural Research Station, also that he was war-time advisor in fruit growing in Kent. However, it did not seem that Herbie and I were to receive any of the great man's advice at first hand, for Harry and Charlie took him off further away from us to discuss the pruning of the young trees.

Later in the day, when Mr. Thompson had left, Harry came and enthusiastically passed on some of the information he had gleaned from him. This was mainly to do with the problems encountered when pruning. For instance, as was well known, when you pruned back a 'leader' the resulting growth from the end bud was stronger that of the lower growths and was often more *upright* than was ideal. On the other hand, the two or three shoots below the cut usually grew at a flatter angle. In order to make use of one of these for extending the branch you could make this shoot grow stronger by cutting out a *notch* in the stem just above it, and also weaken the end shoot by cutting a *nick* in the stem just below it. In the following year you could then cut off the end shoot, and retain the lower one at a better angle, for the branch extension.

I found these ideas fascinating; these *notching* and *nicking* cuts could be used for correcting various problems, including the problem of the uneven growth of the 'leader' shoots, mentioned earlier. Harry continued to refer to Mr. Thompson as 'Professor', though since then I have wondered whether in fact the title of professor had been correct. Harry told us that as well as having been involved in pruning trials, the 'professor' had worked out his own pruning system and was writing a book about it – it was to be called: 'The Pruning of Apples and Pears by Renewal Methods'. This title stuck in my mind for many years afterwards, but it was not until the year 2007 that we got around to finding a copy on the Internet.

Remainder of the Pruning Season

After the young apples had been pruned there were other large apple trees to be dealt with. Owing to the height of some of these, they required the use of ordinary ladders as well as the step-ladders that we used. When these had been completed, I remember we went into an orchard of young pear trees. I found the pruning of these pears to be another quite stimulating job for, just as the young apples had been, these too were in the formative stage of being trained into shape. However, unlike the apples that had been in the form of an open-centred tree, these pears were being grown with a central stem, round which *three tiers* of branches were being trained. We therefore had more variation, giving additional interest to the work. Furthermore, we were also able to practice some of Professor Thompson's *nicking* and *notching* in dealing with any growth that was rather unbalanced, which again provided more fascination for the work. Just why these trees

95

were being grown with the three tiers of branches, I don't know. I can't imagine them being allowed to grow into big trees in that form – perhaps the higher tiers were removed at a later stage treating them as what were known as *delayed-open-centred* trees.

Next came the turn of the various varieties of plum trees to receive attention. Young plum trees in their early stages need a certain amount of training, but not as much as that required by apples and pears. The plum tree seems to form spurs naturally and more readily, so except for cutting back the side growths where they overlap and shade adjacent branches, they are not cut any more than absolutely necessary. The branch *leaders* are cut back for training the branches for one or two years and then, apart from cutting out crossing, or dead wood the trees are left alone. This minimum amount of pruning needed, can often be carried out using the *long-arm* pruners, though I seem to remember having to use ladders for the damson and the greengage trees which were quite tall. Another job remembered was two or three days spent getting up greengage suckers, using the *twivel*. Some of theses suckers were up to about 2 ½ inch diameter, with numerous smaller ones.

Plum and damson trees are susceptible to the Silver-leaf disease, the spores of which are abundant in the winter, so it is best to leave the pruning until the spring where this is possible. With the numbers of trees that we had at Chivers, they could not all be left as long as this, but they would be done as late in the winter and as close to spring as was possible. Branches affected by silver leaf are cut off, back into the healthy wood, and the diseased portions are burned. What I didn't know at the time, but have read since, was that in the 1940s there was a *Silver Leaf Order* of the Ministry of Agriculture, under which all wood affected must be removed and burned by 15th July each year. I do remember, however, Curly on one occasion loading up diseased branches onto his lorry from where they had been cut off the trees and taking them away somewhere – presumably to a suitable place for burning.

Spring-time: Creating a New Orchard

The final job of my first pruning season was to help in an apple orchard that was to have its fruit variety changed, by being grafted. This took place in early April. It is a pity that I cannot now recall what the two apple varieties were. Presumably the variety being sacrificed was one that was no longer in demand, and that the new one was of greater commercial value. The reason for grafting scions of the new variety onto large, established trees was, of course, the fact that a productive orchard could be achieved in much quicker time than by starting off a new orchard with maiden trees. The apple orchard concerned in the project, was on the left-hand side of Cawcutts Farm roadway as you approached the farm. We had not been required to save any pruning material from any of the trees that we had pruned during the winter, so I think that the *scions* that were to be used were brought to Cawcutts by Doug Foster, the propagation man. These scions were prunings that had been saved from trees of the required variety, of about ½ inch diameter and 18 inches long. They were fresh prunings of one-year-old wood. When work started Doug came each day to help and made up a foursome with Charlie, Ken and Herbie; unfortunately I did not get to do any grafting – my job was to treat the grafts with hot grafting-wax.

When Herbie and I had been nearing the end of working on the plums, Harry had told us that our next job would be to take part in the grafting of the orchard at Cawcutts. He also said that my part would be to apply the grafting wax to the base of the scions. Herbie told me a bit about the scions, how they had to be made from fairly fresh prunings that had not dried out; also a little about the grafting process itself: how the scions were shaped to fit into slits made in the branches of the tree. This gave me a rough idea of what to expect but, in my ignorance of the work, nothing of the prior preparation of the trees occurred to me. Thus on my arrival at Cawcutts on the first morning we were to start, I was amazed at the bizarre appearance of the orchard. The branches sticking up round the trunks were completely devoid of any kind of side growths whatsoever; absolutely bare and looking as if struck by some great catastrophe. On thinking about it I realised that of course the trees would have to be cleared of the growth that had previously borne the old variety, in order to give way to the new. But, not having thought about it previously, I had not been prepared for the outlandish and almost ghostly sight of the orchard. It was obvious that whilst Herbert and I had been finishing the plums, Charlie and Ken had been engaged in removing all the side-growths from the trees. Also, that Bill and the women had removed and burnt all the waste, for the ground was now completely clear and ready for the grafting operations to begin.

The weather was very spring-like – quite warm and sunny – and very pleasant in the orchard, which had been grassed down underfoot. The step-ladders we were to use for the job were heavy wooden three-legged ones of about 5 feet tall. They had a two-foot square platform at the top, with a vertical handle extending up from the back of this for support. Unlike the lighter-weight step-ladders we had used in the apples, these did not fold up, and were more like a very tall stool. Harry arrived on the scene while the men were still getting organised, to discuss the work with them; he then took me to show me where the grafting wax had been put, in an old disused brick building. This wax was red in colour, I remember, and Harry explained that it had to be heated up and then applied with a brush while it was still quite warm. He said he would leave it to me to sort out a fire for heating the wax, and that Herbie would show me just how to apply it to the grafts. As usual Harry was in a hurry and he cycled off before I could ask him any questions. I thought that it would have been a good idea if he had supplied me with something in the nature of a *Primus* stove for melting the wax; instead I had to make a fire to do the job.

I found some bricks and arranged them on an open space outside the brick shed to form a surround for a small fire, also as a support on the top to hold the tin of wax for heating. Next was to find a supply of reasonably dry wood for the fire. Luckily for me, Charlie Preston was at the farm and he let me have a quantity of wood from an old shed that he had dismantled. Having got the fire going and heated up the wax to what I thought was a suitable consistency, I took the tin and brush round to the orchard to find Herbie, who showed me how to apply the wax. I now had chance to see what was going on with the grafting. The tool used was the pruning knife and the scions were being cut at one end into a wedge shape of approximately 1 ½ inches in length. A quite deep slit was made in the branch of the tree and the wedge then inserted into this slit, making sure, as Herbie explained, to match up the *cambium* layer just under the bark of the branch with the similar layer of the scion. Unless this careful matching of the layers was done, then the sap of the tree would be unable to connect between the two parts, and the scion would not grow. After the scion had been pushed tightly into place, it was tidied up by cutting a small piece off the end of the lip of the slit. The scions were inserted at oblique angles at regular intervals on alternate sides of each branch, and one could imagine that once they came into leaf, that they would begin to convert the hitherto bare branches into reasonable looking trees once more. All this was hard work on the pruning knives and every so often one or other of the men would re-sharpen his knife.

When each branch had been grafted along its length as described, it was ready for the waxing. I found that with the wax nice and warm, it could be brushed into the spaces on each side of the grafts and then brought round neatly to the front of the graft. In this way, the newly inserted graft would be held in place and the accompanying wound in the branch protected from the weather until it healed. But I soon found that I had a problem: I had not waxed many of the grafts before the wax began to cool and became far too stiff to run into the crevices. I was not very happy about this, for if I could only do such a limited amount of waxing before having to return to the fire, I was not very likely to be able to keep up with the grafting. I returned to the fire and revived it into life and put the tin of wax on top once more. Charlie Preston again came to the rescue; seeing my predicament he suggested that what I needed was a *hay-box*, something I had never heard the use of before. Charlie helpfully found me a wooden box, fixed a wire over the top for a handle, and then suggested I get some hay. I pinched a few handfuls of the Cowman's hay to fill the box and then, when the wax had again heated up, snuggled the tin down in the middle of the hay. This proved to be fairly successful and I was able to wax about three times the number of grafts before re-heating, than my original effort.

Having, with Charlie's help, got myself organised, with the waxing now going well, and enjoying the lovely weather, the morning was very pleasurable. I was in the middle of waxing one of the grafts, my mind in a kind of reverie, when suddenly I was brought back to the present with a jolt, for the steps beneath me started to tip and I grabbed the handle for support. One of the legs of the steps came off the ground – then went down with a bump – then continued in the same fashion for another half-a-dozen jolts. Beneath me was a large white sow, busily rubbing her side against one of the legs of the steps. Each swing of her side as she scratched herself produced a series of lifts and bumps of the steps, with me taken by surprise and clutching my hay-box at the top. Some of the men who had seen all this thought it was hilarious – I suppose it must have looked rather funny. It was quite possible, I thought, that one of them might possibly get caught out in similar fashion, for there were seven or eight of these sows out in the orchard at the time. I got down from the steps, slapped the pig on its rump to move it on and went back to my fire to re-heat the wax.

Having got my fire going again and set the pot of wax to heat up, I wandered into the nearby brick shed to have a look round. Charlie Preston had told me earlier that the shed had at one time been used for apple storage; the method for keeping them had been some kind of gas, he thought, but the shed had not been used for a considerable time. The inside of the shed was divided into a number of separate compartments, I found, but there were no doors between them and I just wandered from one section to another. The atmosphere was gloomy, dark and musty and not very pleasant – a big contrast from the sunshine outside. I was musing on how the method of the gas-storage might have been used in the building when, without warning, a sinister picture filled my mind. Suddenly the dingy brick walls were transformed into the inside of the death camp at Auschwitz. For some time stories of Hitler's atrocities on the Jews had been seeping into Britain and now, in a flash, I saw these unfortunates herded into this very building in which I stood, locked in – and the gas turned on! I was glad to get back to my fire, and the sunshine, and I didn't venture into the shed any more. Gradually, as I worked in the orchard the nightmarish picture faded and I was able to dismiss it from my mind. I carried on with the waxing of the grafted scions and was gradually able to catch up with the grafters and their rather slower and meticulous work. The completion of the grafting brought the pruning season to a close and I wondered what I would be doing next.

Springtime – Helping the Shepherd
Immediately after the grafting was finished Harry asked me to help the shepherd. As I had never seen the shepherd before, I think that he must have been based at one of Chivers' other farms a bit further afield. Harry took me to a cornfield alongside the Cambridge road where the shepherd was *folding* his sheep on the growing corn. What the crop was, whether of wheat, oats or barley, I cannot now recall. But I do remember thinking, in my ignorance, that it seemed to be a strange thing to be feeding the young corn shoots to the sheep, for I thought that this would be the end of the corn crop. However, I later learned that instead of destroying the crop, the sheep would greatly benefit it. The treading of their feet would encourage the young corn to *tiller* – to make new lateral growths from the base of each shoot and so increase the number of stalks that would bear the ears of grain. Furthermore, the droppings left behind by the sheep fertilised the crop.

Most of the season's lambs had already appeared before I arrived on the scene, having been born while I had been engaged on waxing the grafts at Cawcutts. About three-quarters of the cornfield had been eaten by the flock, and there remained a relatively small piece still to be folded. When the area on which the sheep had been feeding was almost eaten down, a fresh enclosure had to be prepared for them. The new enclosure, or *fold*, was made by surrounding it with wooden hurdles. These hurdles were, in effect, portable lengths of fencing, each about 5 feet long and about 3 feet high. They were made of split ash or chestnut, with about six horizontal bars, a diagonal strengthening bar, and an upright piece at each end that extended slightly below the level of the lowest bar and was shaped to a rough point. When these points were knocked a few inches into the ground, they would keep the hurdle in place at the bottom, but the main support was provided by a wooden stake. At one end of each hurdle, about 30 inches above the ground, was an elongated metal ring of about 4 inches by 8 inches. The hurdles, as they were erected, would be slightly overlapped so that the metal ring could be inserted between the bars of the neighbouring hurdle and a post inserted through the ring and knocked into the ground, thus firmly supporting both hurdles at that end. This process was repeated for each hurdle until the required area was enclosed.

As will be understood, the folding of sheep by this method involved the work of moving a lot of hurdles. Sometimes this can be made easier by the use of some transport, such as a pony and lorry, to place small stacks of the hurdles round the field near to where they would be needed. However, on this particular morning it appeared that there was no transport available, so it had to be done by hand; and this of course was where I came in. The shepherd showed me how to carry the hurdles. Taking four hurdles from the pile in the corner of the field, he stood them all together on end, placed the end of one of the wooden posts between the bars, squatted down and placed the post over his shoulder, and then stood up. With the hurdles thus supported on his back, he took them round to where the new enclosure was to begin. I followed his example and got four hurdles supported on my back, but found that it was difficult to position them so that I didn't catch them with the back of my legs as I walked. I threw one of the hurdles down and then tried it with three. Once I got them balanced I found that I could manage them much better – and in any case, three at a time were plenty heavy enough to carry.

I continued back and forth to where the shepherd had stationed himself for the erection of the new enclosure. He had a large wooden mallet, which he used for knocking in the supporting posts between the hurdles. The head of the mallet was supported by two metal bands to prevent it from splitting, but the striking surfaces were wood, which gave less wear and tear on the ends of the posts, than a metal hammer would have done, when they were hammered into the ground. Being a rather slim chap, continually carrying the hurdles made me rather sore from the pressure of the post across my shoulder. However, the shepherd did give me a break at one point; he carried some of the hurdles himself and gave me a go with the mallet. This was a welcome change for a while, but later I was back on carrying hurdles and I was not at all sorry when the erection of the new fold had been completed. The final touch was to fit a *creep* in what had been the boundary of the previous fold, to allow the lambs into the new area so that they could have the 'choice pickings' as it were, before the whole flock was allowed access. A hurdle was removed from the old pen and a lamb creep fitted in its place. Unlike an ordinary hurdle, this had no horizontal bars except at top and bottom, but was made up of perpendicular framing. The upright slats were so spaced that only the lambs could pass between them, thus giving them access to the new crop growth, but also enabling them to get back to their mothers when they wished.

The making of the pen that we had just completed meant that the whole area of the cornfield had now been enclosed and when, finally, the sheep had eaten this off they would have to go elsewhere. As explained, I had not been with the shepherd when the vast majority of the lambs had been born. No doubt he had had some other help at the time, but who this had been I don't know. The sheep were not a permanent feature on Impington Farm so I realised that the shepherd's time on the farm would soon be over. Also, I thought, as all the hard work of making the final pen had now been done, he would not need my services any more. However, there had been a few late lambs born and, before I was to leave him again, I got roped in for helping him with castrating of the ram lambs – not a very pleasant task.

Springtime – Miscellany
After spending two or three days helping with the sheep I was ordered to report on the following day to Harry at the farm once more. Not many days after, whilst cycling home along the Cambridge road I noticed that the sheep had gone. I had not seen anything of them going and had not had any hand in the removal of the hurdles from off the field.

When I arrived at the farm on the morning after finishing with the sheep, Harry said that he wanted me to do some hoeing in the young cabbages. He found me a hoe, which I tied to my bicycle cross-bar, and I cycled off to the cabbage field. By the time I arrived there the other men making up the hoeing gang had already started work, and were part-way into their rows. I took the next row and, by working quickly, managed to bring myself level with the six or seven other men. I suppose that you would describe these men as the farm's *general farm workers.* Unlike the Horsemen, Cowmen and Pigmen who had specific jobs, they were called upon to do all kinds of general work on the farm and spent quite a lot of their time hoeing. Often Harry seemed to use me as a kind of *floating* worker, available to send wherever a bit of extra help was needed, but this did mean that I got to experience quite a lot of different jobs, which was enjoyable. When I joined the men on this particular morning, I was greeted with quite a bit of chaffing. They knew that I often did jobs either with the ponies or the horses, so I was asked whether I had come to *work* for a change, rather than enjoy myself with a *riding* job. This was all harmless banter and I replied in kind, telling them that you had to have *brains* for some jobs and that any *fool* could use a hoe.

To hoe along a few rows of plants in a garden is easy, but to hoe in a field *all day* is hard work. To have to do it *on one's own* would be harder still. To hoe in a gang has a great advantage, the resulting banter, discussions and chit-chat livens things up considerably and makes the time seem shorter. In spite of possible expectations to the contrary, I'm sure that this all helps with the amount of work covered. I recall a number of names of the men in the hoeing gang, though for some only their first names. These were: Ernie, Nobby, Peter and Wally. Wally was a bit of a philosopher and liked to expand on some of his theories and experiences, but I was quite surprised during one of our hoeing days at a remark he made to the other rather rough-and-ready chaps around him. This was to the effect that, as time went by, he appreciated more and more the love and the good qualities of his wife. Wally was a man of about forty-five to fifty years of age and I thought his comment was quite touching.

Another comment of Wally's I have always remembered was: *"Hoe or disturb spring cabbages too soon and they'll bolt, or otherwise run to seed."* This subject no doubt came up because we were hoeing in cabbages at the time, though these were *summer* ones. The other men in the gang were: Ted Newman, Tommy Sewell and Jack Campbell. Jack I had observed on a number of occasions at breakfast in the Big Shed, during my period of horse-leading. I had never seen a man with such deep cracks in his hands, which must have been extremely painful. Jack was a middle-aged bachelor, and I imagined that he probably neglected to look after himself properly, so what with that and the wartime rationing, he was probably short of vitamins and other nutrients to keep his skin in good order.

These men were a lively bunch and I began to enjoy working with them. My only problem was a recurrence of pain in my left shoulder, first caused by the bite I had received from Molly the pony during my spell on the Poultry Farm. I had forgotten all about this, but the constant chopping action with the hoe had brought it back again. However, it was not unbearable so I managed to ignore the pain and the shoulder gradually improved. We all kept abreast of each other in the rows and, in spite of the chattering, we kept up a good steady pace. However, this free-and-easy way of working was to be interrupted. Harry appeared on the horizon on his bike, and as he got closer I heard one or two groans and expletives from some of the men, for it became clear that Harry had brought a hoe with him. This, I was told, was a periodic habit of Harry's and the men knew what to expect – a frantic demonstration of how much ground they should be covering with their hoes. Harry took the next row but instead of starting his hoeing at the near end, he walked down the row until he was level with the gang. He then went at it *hammer and tongs,* at a ridiculously punishing pace that, quite clearly, no one would possibly have been able to keep up all day. The men all felt pressured to keep up with him, so I felt obliged to follow suit, but I thought how silly it looked. I'm sure that if the men had stuck together in hoeing at a reasonable pace, then Harry's actions would have been made to appear as absurd as they actually were. But this didn't happen. Instead we all kept up this gruelling pace until one of the men managed to find time to look at his watch and find that it was 1 o'clock, dinner time. Everyone then promptly dropped their hoes and walked off the field to find their dinner bags.

Harry, kept up the pace for about an hour, but then went off on his bike and didn't return, so we were back to normal again. He had always appeared a perfectly reasonable man in every other way, and I had not realised that he had this occasional, but tiresome habit of annoying the hoeing gang. I stayed on the hoeing for three or four days until the cabbage field was done and then I was sent with Boxer, one of the horses, to horse-hoe the strawberries. The rest of the gang were also transferred, with their hand hoes, into the strawberries and we continued with our respective cleaning operations up to about the end of May. We had to stop then, for in early June the strawberries would begin to ripen and also, before long, it would be time for the pickers to arrive and make a start on them. As I was still in close proximity to the hoeing gang chaps, I couldn't resist pointing out to the ones who, when I'd first joined them, had teased me about my *riding* jobs, that although I was back working with a horse, I was walking behind a horse-hoe – *not riding.* At the end of my horse-hoeing interval Harry dropped an unexpected bombshell: he was going to put me in charge of the records for the fruit-picking gang for the forthcoming season. On thinking about this I realised that I would be on this job from early June until possibly into October, which meant that I would miss out on other jobs that I had looked forward to, particularly the hay-making.

My Short Hay-making Season
But, as I had found before when I had been given jobs that I thought less interesting, there were usually other compensations, and it was all new experience, so I reconciled myself to the idea of being the fruit *Bookie*, as the job had become known. Although I was not to see very much of the hay-making this year, I managed to take part in it for a very short spell before the fruit work started. The main hayfield was to be what we knew as the *Forty-acre*, a field, as the name implies, of 40 acres and which I think was the biggest field on the farm. However, before I got involved on the Forty-acre, I was sent with Old George to a very small grass field at the side of Oswald's Road, which George was to cut with his horse team and grass-cutter. As George went round the field with the cutter, my job was to keep a spare set of cutter blades sharpened for him. The cutting part of the mower was made up of numerous, 4 inch wide triangular blades, all riveted side by side onto a

bar of about five feet long, to give one long cutting tool. The blades each had two cutting edges and the bar on which they were held, moved with a reciprocating action, driven by the land wheels of the mower. This action moved the blades about 6 inches at a time from side to side between a series of metal fingers. The grass, trapped between the blades and the fingers by the forward motion of the mower, was cut off and left in a swath behind the mower. The width of the cut swath would be a little less than the cutting length of the knife bar, by being directed inwards slightly, away from the un-cut grass, by a wooden swath-board fixed at the end of the bar. Thus a clear strip is left for the off-side horse to walk on, and also for the off-side mower wheel to run on.

To support the length of the cutting *knife* while I sharpened the individual triangular blades, I had a wooden trestle with four splayed legs, and a narrow top on which the knife-bar could be firmly held by two metal clamps. The blades were then dealt with by using a metal file to sharpen the two cutting edges on each blade. Each cut round the field by George with the mower produced quite a bit of wear on the blades, so he would stop near me after a round or two in order to exchange the worn knives for the ones I had sharpened for him. It took quite a while to sharpen all the blades along the length of the cutter bar, so I had to keep going to ensure that the sharpened one was ready to exchange as soon as he came round to me. Sharp blades made a great difference to the amount of work required from the horses, far less than when the blades were getting blunt. We carried on like this until the whole of the small field had been cut, then left the hay in the swaths to begin to dry. I expect that the swathed grass would have been *turned* on the following day, to help with the drying process, but I had no more to do with this particular field.

In the meantime grass cutting was also going on in the *Forty Acre*; this would have been done by Edgar, the head horseman and his team, and probably assisted by another horseman and team with an additional mower. The day after, David Peck, one of the horse-men, and I were ordered by Harry to take a horse and a side-delivery rake each from the farm to the hay field and to start turning the swaths. The grass had been cut across the whole field, with the swaths laying in row after row, and it looked quite a large area of work ahead of us. We were a few days into the beginning of June, and fortunately the weather was dry and sunny – just right for hay-making. It was now a case of driving the horse and rake along each row to turn the swaths of hay. The machine was constructed with rows of metal tines that revolved round and round, and down into the swath to lift it and fluff it up somewhat, before returning it to the ground virtually along the same line it had occupied before being turned. This allowed the air to get into the hay to speed up the drying process. We carried on with the turning all day and then, anxious to get the field done, Harry asked us to stay on, which we did (with no tea!) until about 8 pm.

The following day the hay was obviously drying nicely for we were asked to *row it up*. The rake was now adjusted so that the tines would throw each swath out sideways; hence the name *Side-delivery Rake*. This meant that we could merge three or four swaths into one bigger row. The weather was warm but very breezy, ideal for drying the hay quickly, but the strong breeze, I remember, could be rather a nuisance when the rake was working against it, tending to blow the hay back slightly against the direction in which you were moving it. About 10 o'clock in the morning Harry sent about half a dozen men to start heaping up the hay. These were Polish men who used to work on the farm; I didn't know very much about their circumstances, but think that they were possibly refugees from the war. Using two-tined forks they worked their way along our rows of hay, heaping it up into big heaps which were then ready to be collected up by the *horse-sweeps* that would take them to the corner of the field where the hay was to be stacked.

The *sweeps* were about 8 feet wide, propelled by a horse harnessed at each side, who were driven by the horseman from a seat in the middle at the rear. Spaced at intervals of about 1 foot, across the whole width of the implement were wooden splines of about 6 feet long, projecting forward just above ground level. The two horses would be driven, one each side, to the heaps of hay, pushing the wooden splines beneath the heap and thereby collecting the hay above the splines. As the splines were pushed into the heaps, the hay would come to rest against a back-board on the implement, and could then be transported across the field to the stack. It was possible, depending on the size of the heaps, to load more than one heap onto the implement, and the transport to the stack by this method was much quicker than having to load the hay onto wagons. David Peck and I continued rowing up that day and I recall that it was another long day – we finished the field sometime in late evening. This was to be the last of my input into the hay-making process that year, for fruit picking time had come.

Fruit Picking Season – I become 'Fruit Bookie'

We were now about a week into June 1946, and on the morning that we were to start strawberry picking Harry gave me initial instructions concerning my new fruit-recording job. The opening of the picking season had been advertised locally, so it was expected that a number of the regular casual workers, who took part from year to year, would turn up this first day. However, not knowing how many of these would come, Harry said that he was going to send about five of the farm men to help pick.

Harry had an order from Covent Garden Market for 1,000 chips of strawberries from this first day's picking and he wanted to be sure that this number would be achieved. He supplied me with a thick hard-backed, foolscap sized, notebook. In this I was to take the names and addresses of the fruit pickers as they arrived and to issue each one of them with a number. The names and addresses would be recorded at the back of the book. Columns were to be ruled in the front of the book, headed numerically at the top with the pickers' allocated numbers. These columns were to be used for recording the individual weights picked by each person, as the payment would be on a *piece-work* basis of so much per pound weight of fruit picked. I was then sent off with Curly and his pony and lorry with a load of *chip baskets* and the weighing machine that I was to use for the job, to prepare for the coming of the pickers.

When we arrived at the strawberry field, Bill Butler and his three regular farm women, Doris, Rene and Olly, were already there. Bill, was well used to the set-up for the fruit season, for he was the one put in charge of looking after and supervising the picking gang. Later, when the picking of the *top-fruit* began he would move the ladders for them. I found that Bill had already set up a seat for me, composed of a pile of upside-down Chivers wooden fruit trays, and another tray on which to stand the weighing machine.

Strawberry Picking at Chivers
(Photograph courtesy of the Cambridgeshire Collection)

Doris, Rene and Olly, were well-known as the *champion* fruit pickers. They were itching to get started, but as they had not had any baskets until Curly and I arrived, they had not been able to. Bill cut the strings on one of the bundles of chip baskets for them; they grabbed about four baskets each and headed off into the strawberries. As I was to find later, they really were the champions. Hardly anyone else got close to them for the speed at which they could pick and, during the season, they were able to earn considerably more than their normal weekly farm wages. One thing they never seemed to learn though. Whenever the picking of one crop had finished – for example, passing onto gooseberries after finishing the strawberries – Harry would not set the price for the new crop for a day or two. He would wait to see how much the three women could pick and then base the price on that. Bill used to warn them not to rush madly into the picking at first, but to wait until they knew the price, otherwise it would be set a bit lower than otherwise it would have been. But the speed they set themselves seemed to be built into their psyche – they couldn't help themselves.

Bill and I had our breakfasts at the usual time of 9 o'clock and by the time we had finished, various people, mostly women, started arriving for the fruit picking. I think that they were mainly housewives, some having taken their children to school, and now come to take the opportunity of earning some extra cash. Most of them had been in previous years and knew what to expect and, seeing me with the book, came to give their names and addresses and to be allocated a number. During this first influx of people, Bill took charge of untying the bundles of chip baskets and issuing these, and then starting each individual into the end of a strawberry row, explaining as he did so that it was only the ripe ones that were to be picked.

I was kept busy for a while taking names and issuing the numbers as more people arrived. In addition to the regular farm staff, we eventually had about 20 *casual* people arrive at the field, so in all there were about 28 pickers during that first day. After a while, when the earliest pickers had filled their baskets they began arriving at my weighing machine to have their pickings recorded. The weighing scales had large round perpendicular face with an indicator, rather like the minute hand on a clock, to show the weight, and a flat metal tray on top, on which the chip baskets were placed. The pickers would call out their allotted number and I would record the weight of the fruit in the appropriate column in my book.

Another job that had to be done was to adjust the amount of strawberries in the chip baskets so that they each contained the required weight of 2 lbs. To do this, a second weighing machine, a *balance* machine with separate brass 2-lb weight, plus smaller ones to allow for the weight of the basket, was used. This second machine was set up on another pile of up-turned fruit trays a short distance away from my seat. Once a picker had weighed up their baskets and had them recorded on my weighing machine, the baskets would then be set down in a stack next to the second machine ready for their individual checking. Once this check-weighing had been done the baskets were stacked separately ready for later collection. With a relatively few number of pickers on the first day, I was able to carry out this second weighing, in addition to my main job of recording for the pickers. However, soon after, as the number of pickers considerably increased, I was kept much busier and we then had to have an additional man for this job.

A further need was to remove the strings that held the bundles of empty chip baskets, so that there were plenty of empties available and the pickers were not held up. These strings were quite thick, and I found that if I cut them close to the knots, they would come off the bundles in quite long lengths. I started to carefully save these strings, thinking that they would be useful for the tying up of plum branches – a job I had previously helped with. I managed to save a considerable quantity of the strings, and when I suggested to Harry that they could be used for the plums, he seemed highly delighted, and we did in fact use them for that purpose.

Some of the women left off at about 3.30 p.m. in order to collect children from school; some stayed on until about 4.30 when the picking was timed to finish. We ended up with a total of just over 1,100 x 2 lb. chips of strawberries, so Harry's aim of 1,000 chips for the Covent Garden was achieved. The following day quite a number of further pickers arrived and later on the picking gang swelled to over 60 pickers. I was much surprised how, eventually, with the continual weighing and recording, I was able to put a number to a face and get to remember nearly all of them. For a short time at first, some of the pickers would forget their own number and ask me to check what it was.

The 'Fruit Bookie' - Weighing Blackcurrants for the Pickers
(Photograph courtesy of the Cambridgeshire Collection)

On the whole the pickers were a cheery lot of people; there was a great deal of light banter and repartee that went on, and many of them treated the job as a kind of holiday.

The strawberry picking went on until about the middle of July, but before it was finished the gooseberries were also ready for picking, so we had days alternating between the two. As gooseberries are so much firmer than strawberries and can stand much rougher treatment, they were picked into larger *wicker* baskets, each with a carrying handle, and with two baskets at a time allocated to each picker. The baskets were quite heavy when full and so to carry one in each hand when taking them up to be weighed, was a much more balanced way to do it.

These two baskets were of such a size that the two could just be accommodated, side by side, on the flat plate of the weighing machine, so that I could weigh them both together. The baskets, being made of *wickerwork* were fairly heavy, so allowance had to be made for this when recording the amount of fruit picked. Before the crop was started on, a number of the empty baskets would be weighed and an average weight arrived at. This amount would be deducted at each weighing.

Gooseberries are not so easy to pick as strawberries owing to the thorns on the bushes, and the most of the pickers would therefore be very careful how they picked. This resulted in a very nice-looking sample of gooseberries containing very few leaves. This method of picking though was not fast enough for our three 'regulars', Doris, Rene and Olly; they had their own technique! Whereas other people would carefully pick the gooseberries one at a time, avoiding the thorns, Doris & Co., each wearing some thick gloves, would grasp a gooseberry branch and then drawing their hands towards them, would remove a dozen or more gooseberries at a time. This would result in a great many *leaves* being put into the baskets, as well as the fruit. When their baskets were full and ready for weighing, they would endeavour to improve the look of the baskets by quickly removing as many leaves as possible from the surface.

Bill had warned me about this practice, so I was prepared. Now and again, when he was around, Bill would tell them off for it, but most of the time I think he turned a *blind eye*. Occasionally when they came to weigh up, just to make the point, I would refuse to do the weighing until they tipped each basket-full of gooseberries into another basket and picked out some of the leaves. I would tell them that as well as stripping off the gooseberries, they were removing a lot of the buds of next year's crop. They regarded me as a *pain!*

When the picking of strawberries and gooseberries came to an end, there was a bit of a lull as far as fruit-picking was concerned, until the *Early Rivers* plums were ripe, so in the interim I was given various other jobs. I helped to tie up the plum trees, such as the *Victorias* and the *Czars,* had a spell of cabbage cutting, also of picking up potatoes and, of course the usual puncture repairs on Harry's bike. Then the early blackcurrants began to ripen, so picking started on these and once again I became busy with the fruit recording. There were quite a lot of blackcurrants and, with the different varieties, the picking lasted a considerable time. In between this, the *Early Rivers* were ready. On our first go at these, we were picking them over to select the ripest ones, but after a day or two they were all ready and we were able to *strip* the trees. Towards the end of July and into August, there were other plums to pick; then at the end of August, the greengages. Following these came the damsons. The fruit picking, the weighing up and the loading up of fruit, now went on non-stop and everyone involved was kept very busy.

In the August, other fruit that began to ripen was the blackberries on the poultry farm. These were the ones that Herbie and I had pruned during the previous autumn. We now had a number of spells on these, picking them over as they ripened. The blackberries, like the strawberries, were picked into chip baskets and we had another young lad to help with the weighing of these to get them to the correct weight. I am particularly reminded of a rather comical little incident that happened during the blackberry season. One of the pickers was a rather elderly foreign lady, quite small and rather thin with rather a gaunt looking face, though very lively and cheerful. This lady used to smoke cigarettes. As she found it difficult to pick the blackberries and smoke at the same time, she got into a routine of weighing up her fruit and then, on returning to her blackberry row, would sit down at the end of the row to have a smoke before starting work again. One afternoon, after having recently weighed up, she suddenly appeared back at the scales in great distress. Gesticulating rather wildly, she pointed at the accumulating stack of baskets that our young helper had dealt with and cried: "My teeth are in there!!" Apparently, each time she stopped to have her smoke, she used to take out her false teeth for comfort, and lay them in one of her chip baskets. On the last occasion she had forgotten to put them back in her mouth, had covered them with blackberries, and then weighed up. We must have transferred about 40 or 50 baskets of blackberries into fresh baskets before finding the teeth. It was worth it, just to see the relief on the old lady's face!

My Fruit Recording Continues – but with Distractions.
As the season progressed and we had got up to 60 - 70 pickers, there was little change in their makeup. A few came for a short while and then left, but these were usually compensated for by the arrival of a few fresh faces. A couple of schoolboys came during the August holidays, to earn themselves some pocket money. I must also mention a newcomer who had arrived during the picking of the *Early Rivers* and had particularly caught my attention. Most of the pickers were housewives and mothers with school children, but this new arrival was a very attractive young lady of about my own age. I was quite smitten! She had a pretty face, blonde hair, and wore a coloured blouse and some navy-blue slacks, I remember.[5] I was very attentive as I took down her details, issued the picking number, found her some baskets, and then directed to where I thought she would find Bill Butler, telling her that Bill would show her where to start picking. I then watched as this vision of femininity walked into the trees and out of sight, and much looked forward to seeing her again shortly. I had not had any problem with finding out her name of course, for it was one of the details I had had to record in my book. It was *Zoe,* and she lived in Histon.

---

[5] *This was probably in the 1947 season.*

*Carting fruit – probably plums destined for the Histon factory
(Photograph courtesy of the Cambridgeshire Collection)*

During the picking of the plums and, later, the apples, a lot of ladder moving was required and Bill Butler was kept very busy attending to the Pickers and moving their ladders for them. The bulk of the fruit orchards were grouped in the area that we used to refer to as '*down the fen'*. When one variety of plum or apple had been picked and we had to move onto another variety, it was quite a performance. If the fresh section was fairly close by, Bill and I, and whoever else was helping at the time, would move all the ladders by hand in order to get the picking started again without delay, and then set up the weighing machines in the new position. In this case the pickers would each carry their empty baskets across to the new variety. Harry would keep in touch with our daily progress and whenever we had to move he would send a fresh set of the containers to us by one of the pony lorries. These containers, wooden trays, wooden boxes or wicker skeps, would be stacked up ready for use in the vicinity of the scales.

However, when we had to move greater distances, say from Impington Farm to one of the other farms, it was a bigger operation. The transport would be carried out on the pony lorries, usually by Curly and another of the pony boys. The weighing machines, plus all the 100-plus wicker baskets would be loaded onto one lorry, with strings threaded through the handles of the outside ones to stop any of them falling off in transit.

The ladders would be loaded onto the other lorry, with one end of each ladder protruding over the front board of the lorry, on each side of the driving seat, and the other ends sticking out at the rear. Curly would have to clamber over the loaded ladders to reach his driving seat, and he used to look rather strange sitting between the piles of ladders on either side of him. He would usually have to make more than one trip to transport all the ladders.

The majority of the Pickers used to arrive for work on their bicycles, so they and the rest of the staff used to cycle to the fresh picking site. When the equipment had all been taken to the new site, one of the pony lorries would return to collect the Pickers who had no cycles. One of these longer-distance moves would be to the poultry farm, to pick the Victoria plums there. Other moves were to Cawcutts farm, also to Park farm, where there were a considerable number of apple trees. Some other trees we had to pick were in a smaller site situated on the left of the Cambridge road, just before you reached the Histon station level crossing. Here was an old windmill and cottage, within a private garden. Whether the property belonged to the Chivers family, or whether the occupants just had an agreement for us to pick the fruit, I don't know. I remember it as being a very enclosed and attractive garden.

Bill Butler, and 'Curly' standing on his Pony Lorry
(Photograph – Author)

At the end of each day's picking I used to take my record book to the farm and sit in Harry's little office to total up the columns of the individual weights that had been picked during the day. During the day and the actual picking, I was usually too busy with weighing up the fruit and attending to other requirements, such as setting out the containers for the Pickers to empty their fruit into, after their wicker baskets had been weighed and recorded. Sometimes, if I had a spare moment I would do a bit of *sub-totalling* in the book, so as to reduce the amount of totalling up needed at the end of the day, but most of it would of necessity be left until I got to the office. From my book, Harry would make a note of the daily weights for each of the Pickers, and add these to their *running totals*, and thus keep an up-to-date record in the office ready for making up the payments at the end of the week.

As the days went by and Zoë continued to come, my interest in her intensified. Each time she arrived at the scales to weigh up, in spite of an inherent shyness on my part, I managed to get her chatting. She didn't seem averse to this; in fact each time she brought her fruit to the scales, she seemed to get to expect it, and the chatting became a habit between us. I learned that she had a regular job as an usherette at the *Victoria* Cinema in Cambridge, which involved mainly evening work; hence she was able to come fruit picking to earn some extra cash. Sometimes, when I saw her approaching with her laden baskets of fruit, if no one else was waiting to weigh up, I would dash into the trees to meet her and carry the baskets for her and put them on the scales. Occasionally when I did this, when I turned back towards the scales I would find that another woman had approached from a different direction and was waiting to have her baskets weighed. Depending on who it was, she would either be annoyed at having to wait for me, or she would be amused at my obvious attraction to Zoë. It wasn't long before it became clear that some of the women had commented to each other on the subject, and they began to pull my leg about it.

'Digger'
Although almost all the pickers were women, in addition to the one or two boys who were with us, a slightly older young man had started during the plum picking and then stayed on right through the apple

120

harvest. He was an Australian in his early twenties, so of course he soon became known and referred to as *'Digger'*. Digger was quite a character, cheerful and full of jokes with every one.

Plum Picking and Ladder Moving
(Photograph courtesy of the Cambridgeshire Collection)

Digger would be quietly picking for some time, but then, suddenly he would be at the top of his ladder, looking out from the top of his tree and start up a loud monologue that could be heard right across the orchard. His favourite was an impersonation of a cockney costermonger, either:*"Shan't be rarned termorrer – the wheel's come orf me barrer"*, or the rather less salubrious: *"Shan't be rarned termorrer – the donkey's wee'd all over the strawberries"*. Another one was: *" I've stood on this market for fifty years. We're not 'ere terday and gorn termorrer – nah, we'er orf ternight."*

Then he would start to sing; a favourite was:
> *"And when I die, don't bury me at all,*
> *Just pickle my bones in alcohol,*
> *Put a bottle of rum at my head and feet*
> *And bury me where the vines grow deep!"*

Digger had the sense not to annoy people by keeping this up for too long; he would give just the one rendition and then all would go quiet again. He certainly livened things up and I thought him hilarious.

Digger was not really such a crude chap as his sayings and songs suggest. I think that he was in the UK for a holiday. Whether he had any relations anywhere over here I don't know, but during his fruit picking time at Chivers he was living in lodgings in Parker Street in Cambridge. When I told him, one day, that his lodgings were only a short distance from where I lived in Eden Street, he suggested that we could meet sometime and go out for an evening. Although he was perfectly happy during the daytime at Chivers, he knew no one in Cambridge and said that his evenings could be rather boring. We both looked through the Cambridge newspaper to see what films were advertised for the week and, after agreeing on which one we would like to see, we met one evening and went to the pictures. I think it was the cinema in Regent Street, but what the actual film was I have long since forgotten. We went back to his lodgings after the film, where his landlady kindly made us some tea. Digger, in his usual way, was full of fun and the telling of jokes and, all in all the evening made a nice change, giving us both a bit of companionship.

A Bigger Attraction

An evening out with Digger, though pleasant, was not quite the kind of companionship for which I was really longing, and my thoughts during this period were continually turning to Zoë. How, I wondered, could I get to see more of her? During our short daytime chats I began asking her about her job at the Victoria cinema and about the current films that were being shown. Then, when there was a film on that sounded interesting, after ascertaining that she would be on duty, I said that I would go to see the film on such and such an evening. She said that she would look out for me. When one first enters a cinema it is not at first easy to see clearly in the dimmed light, so I wondered whether I would be met by some other usherette. But, true to her word, Zoë met me when I arrived and escorted me to a seat at the rear of the cinema, a little way in from the gangway. She told me that she would see me later, before the end of the programme. About twenty minutes before the end of the last film, she suddenly appeared and sat down beside me. I was thrilled. I had not been taking much notice if the film anyway, for my thoughts had been upon her – and now, here was Zoë sitting next to me. At the end of the evening's programme, Zoë told me that it would take her a few minutes to get her coat and to collect her bicycle, so I said that I would wait for her outside.

I went out of the cinema amongst the general throng of people, but as they all dispersed to go their separate ways, I waited on Market Hill for Zoë. After a few minutes she emerged, with her bicycle, from a side door of the cinema. I took the bicycle and wheeled it for her as we started to walk out of the town, chatting as we went along. Most of the conversation, I must confess, came from Zoë for I was my usual diffident self, though I enjoyed walking with her immensely. We walked out of town, along Hobson Street and King Street and then along the length of Victoria Avenue, I remember, to what was then known as Mitcham's Corner. Here we said goodnight, and Zoë mounted her bike for the rest of her journey home. I walked cheerfully homewards, happy that I had now met Zoë away from the context of work.

The following week I repeated my visit to the cinema and, as before, Zoë came and sat with me. This time, overcoming my shyness, I took her hand in mine and we sat holding hands for the rest of the film. Afterwards we took the same route out of town, but instead of leaving her at Mitcham's Corner as before, we continued walking; a short distance along Milton road we turned left into Gilbert Road and walked through to Histon Road. Eventually, oblivious of time, we came to the far end of Arbury Road, on the outskirts of Histon, before she decided that she would cycle. Plucking up all my courage, I asked her if she would give me a kiss. She jokingly replied something to the effect that she *thought it would be all right, as she knew me*, and I gave her a very shy kiss, before saying goodnight and watching her cycle off home. Being still in rather a whirl after kissing those rosy lips, I absently pressed my handkerchief to my own, and then realised that I had transferred a bright lipstick stain to the handkerchief. I walked home as though on *cloud nine*, with the handkerchief in my pocket as a memento and feeling that our relationship was getting somewhere at last.

During our walk towards Histon, Zoë had told me that she would not be coming to the fruit picking for the next couple of weeks, as she was going away with her parents, but that she would see me afterwards. They say that *the course of true love never runs smoothly*, and so it was to be. Unluckily, during the second week of Zoë's absence the apple picking came to an end – the fruit season was over – and Zoë didn't come any more. With the expectation of seeing each other on her return, we had not made any different arrangements. Although details of her address were in the fruit record book, the book had now gone back to Harry, and I didn't feel that I could ask him for it. I dithered for some time, not making up my mind on a course of action, until at last I decided on trying another visit to the Victoria cinema to see if I could contact Zoë when she left off. I waited outside on Market Hill. However, I had noticed another young chap, who had a bicycle, waiting near the cinema's side door, so I moved away slightly to watch, hoping against hope that he was not waiting for Zoë. When Zoë emerged through the door with her bike, my worst fears were confirmed. It was now over a month since I had seen her and there had obviously been new developments. From the way she and the young man greeted each other, it was quite clear that this was nothing like a casual acquaintance, and I was devastated. It would not have been fair on Zoë for me to barge in, and soon they mounted their bikes and rode off without noticing me.

That was the last time I saw Zoë. It is said that *'Faint heart never wins fair lady'* and that was certainly my experience. I think my problem, deep down, was the feeling that such a stunning girl could never really be interested in *me*. If I had been more positive and not so shy, and had read the signs aright perhaps things could have been different. For, after all, she had habitually chatted to me at work; had been happy to walk and talk with me when she could have been cycling home; had willingly held my hand in the cinema and, finally, had given me a kiss! That, then is the story of my rather short-lived romantic interlude; not strictly on the subject of *work*, but it nevertheless had to be told, for it was all part of my *Chivers experience*. But again, as is said, things often turn out for the best. Although the experience was an extremely painful one, and took a while to recover from, it *was* probably a good thing that I did not get to settling down at such an early age. When I eventually married I was twenty-five years of age; I married the best wife in the world, and now, in the year 2,008, we have been together for 55 years, we have a wonderful family, and no regrets!

Back to Work
The foregoing portrait of my work at Chivers has, for the purpose of a continuous narrative, brought us to about the end of October 1946. However, as explained earlier, although my descriptions of the jobs I have done have been described as accurately as possible, they are not all drawn from just one year, but from two or three years. I was engaged on pruning work for three years running, and also recorded the weights picked by the fruit gang for two separate fruit seasons. During the year 1947 I kept up daily diary entries of my work for part of the year – which was rather a novelty, for I did not do so in any of the other years. Unfortunately I left out virtually the whole of the fruit picking period, which was a pity for it could have given me the exact dates of picking for all the different varieties of fruit.

The winter of 1946-47 was very cold and the snow seemed to hang about for weeks on end; it was the most uncomfortable pruning season that I experienced as far as weather was concerned. The following diary entries give some idea of the conditions:-

Sat.28 Dec: *Fetched water for Park Farm horse-keeper and Mr Wrycroft.*

Tues.7 Jan: *Sorting potatoes in potato shed from 2.30pm owing to heavy fall of snow*

Tues.4 Feb: *Pruning pears until about 3 pm – Snow.*

Wed.19 Feb: *To blacksmiths to fetch draw-bar and frost studs.*

Thurs.20 Feb: *Cawcutts – thawed out pipes in tank house; lagged them With bags of straw*

Fri.21Feb   *Pruning Damsons until dinnertime – Snow – cleared up in barn*

Mon.24 Feb: *Very cold in morning.*

Wed.5 Mar: *Difficult cycling to work; Snowed on and off all day. Car half off road in snowdrift on Stanley's Road*

Thurs.6 Mar: *Not at work owing to heavy fall of snow during the night*

Sat.8 Mar: *Met Reg Pettit with two scrapers in Arbury Road, Helped him, B. Butler, Nobby, Tommy Sewell and Wally, to clear snow from gateway, down to Dumas House.*

Thurs.13 Mar: *Cleaning and painting ladders in Big Shed, owing to rain.*

    Ditch overflowing and flooding orchards. FR, KF and WB cutting channels to take the water off. Should have been done in the morning (across bridge, and not at the sides where they made them)

Obviously the snow was now beginning to melt. The flooding referred to in the last entry above was the only problem this caused on Impington farm at Histon. But, at the same time, in the Cambridge-shire and Isle of Ely fens, river-banks were bursting and thousands of acres were being flooded, with extensive destruction of property, in the well-known 1947 Floods.

Cultivating in the Blackcurrants
(Photograph courtesy of the Cambridgeshire Collection)

I continued working for Chivers, based at Impington Farm, until about the June of 1948 and, for the greater part of my time there, I enjoyed every minute of my involvement. Here then ends the telling of my *'Chivers Experience'*, which I trust will prove of interest and will serve to give some idea of what it was like to work on a farm in the 1940s.

----------ooOoo----------

Part 2.

Diary Entries 1947
by Cyril Marsters
whilst working on Chivers Farms at Histon, Cambs.

NB.: The basic working week was 48 hours in 5½ days.
Hours of work: 7am-5pm (summer), 7am-4.30pm (winter)
Meal Breaks: Breakfast ½ hour at 9am; Dinner 1 hour at 1pm(summer), ½ hour(winter)

In some cases the farm staff are referred to in the Diary simply by their initials;
These are as follows:-

C.C.	= Charlie Camps	C.N.	= C. Newman
C.W.	= Charlie Wrycroft	F.R.	= Fred Reeder
H.C.	= Harry Chambers	H.H.	= Herbert Hankin
K.F.	= Ken Fishpool	O.	= Ollie

W/E. Jan. 4. 1947

Sat.28. (Dec.'46) Turned wheat in Arbury corn shed. Got out brown pony; walked to Cawcutts and unloaded lorry of pig manure. Load of hay [from] 'Gap' to Park Farm. Water for horse-keeper and Mr. Wrycroft (pipes frozen up). Bag of clover seed – 'Gap' to Impington Farm.

Mon.30. Pruning greengages with H. Hankin at Park Farm. I went to workshop about 12 o'clock for new blade to be put in 'long-arm' pruners.

Tues.31. Pruning gages until breakfast time. To Impington Farm to clear up loft and tool shed after breakfast, owing to rain. Back on gages after dinner.

Wed.1.1947. Pruning greengages at Park Farm with H. Hankin. I went to farmyard after breakfast to get a bag of straw, then lit a fire for the women to burn some of the gage wood.

Thur.2. Pruning gages with H. Hankin at Park Farm.

Fri. 3. Ditto as Thursday. Messrs Chambers and Wrycroft brought wages about 12.30pm.

Sat. 4. Ditto "   "   Mr. Chambers came about 12 noon and decided which Yellow Egg trees were to be pulled up. We marked these trees by slicing off some bark on two sides of the trunks.

Mon.6.   Finished pruning the gages about 8.30am. Started pruning the Yellow Eggs. Sid. Star came and cut off the tops of the ones to be pulled up. I took our two pruning saws, and two that C. Camps and K. Fishpool were using, to the carpenters' shop and had them sharpened during the morning. Went with Mr Wrycroft to the apple shed and helped him take some baskets of apples to the Estate Office.

Tues.7.   Pruning apples and plums on the 'plots' at Cawcutts with H. Hankin and F. Reeder.

Sorting potatoes in Arbury potato shed from 2.30pm owing to heavy snowfall.

Wed.8.   Went with Bruno the German prisoner and got a load of barley straw from Hammond's field, to Cawcutts (for pigs). Another load to the farm, which we spread in the yards.

Load of hay from back of Woodhouse (the 40 Acre) to Cawcutts for the cows.

Fed the pony and took the 'roughs' out of his shoes. Note: Food for pony – 2 sieves of chaff, 1 bowl oats, ½ bushel mangolds. Only stopped for 10 minutes for dinner which was at 2.45pm.

Thur.9.   Pruning single row Red Eggs, in front of 'Nursery Shed' with H. Hankin until about 2.30pm, when Mr Wrycroft came and we started pruning the young apples on Mansfield. F. Reeder was with us until breakfast time, after which he went spraying.

Fri.10.   Pruning the row of Red Eggs opposite 'Nursery Shed' with H. Hankin. Mr Chambers and Mr Wrycroft brought money about 10.30am. NB: Red Egg wood fairly tough to cut; sprained my wrist today. I lit fires for breakfast and dinner.

Sat.11.   Called at 'Nursery Shed' to get long-arms and saws, then went to the 'plots' at Cawcutts to continue pruning the apples and plums.

Mon.13.   Pruning on 'plots'. Spread some manure in front of Edgar, who was ploughing. Finished 'plots' about 2 pm and went back to 'Nursery Shed.' Rain. On the Red Eggs until 4.30pm.

Tue.14.   Pruning Red Eggs. Went to Surgery. *[the surgery at the factory – probably to have my wrist bandaged]*. Had one

	saw sharpened and long-arms repaired (wire shortened). Pruning young apples in Mansfield from 11.30am.
Wed.15.	Pruning Red Eggs; started on double row about 11 am. Went to Clinic. Had 1 saw sharpened.
Thur.16.	Pruning Red Eggs until 11.30 am when we went on apples with C. Wrycroft 'till 4.30.
Fri. 17.	Red Eggs all Day. Brought money about 10.30 am.
Sat.18.	Absent owing to wrist, and Mum not well.

W/E.Jan.25.1947

Mon.20.	Pruning Red Eggs until 11.30 am; Mr Chambers asked me to collect the cutting and put on Sid Star's fire (Sid is other side of Hammond's hedge, burning). On apples for the rest of the day.
Tue.21.	Pruning Red Eggs all day.
Wed.22.	Ditto.
Thur.23.	Ditto. Top off hay stack with Curly. On Apples until 4.30 pm.
Fri.24.	Ditto. Money 10.30 am. Finished apples after dinner. Red Eggs again 3.30–4.30 pm
Sat.25.	Finished Red Eggs 12 noon. Pulled out some wood to make up time.

W/E.Feb.1.1947

Mon.27.	Started on pears near 'Nursery Shed' with Herbert. 12 noon Chambers and Wrycroft came. I went to farm to repair puncture in H.C's bike. Five punctures in front tube; hole in cover; oiled chain, adjusted back brake. Back on pears 'till 4.30 pm. Muddle!
Tue.28.	Pruning pears until 12 o'clock. Wen to farm for ticket, and white-lead paint tin and brush. Thawed them out at Cawcutts mess-hut and then got 2 lbs paint from factory. Took it to Nursery Shed , ready to paint the pears where tops are being taken out.. Pruning until 4.30 pm.
Wed.29.	Burning hedge cuttings, top of field 34, until dinner. Painted four rows of pears, 'til 2.30 pm; pruning until 4.30 pm.
Thur.30.	Burning, top of 32, until dinner. Pruning pears until 4.30 pm.
Fri.31.	Burning until breakfast. Pruning rest of the day. (Painted four rows of pears after dinner) Money about 11.50 am.
Sat.1.	Finished burning this side of hedge about 11 am. Pulled out, cut up and put in heaps, ready for burning wood on other side (in corner).

Mon.3.	Pruning pears until 10 am. Rain. Sent to Apple Shed with F. Reeder and Olive. Sorting apples until 4.30pm. Curly took 15 trays of speckled ones in afternoon. I bought one tray – 2 shillings.
Tues.4.	Pruning pears until about 3 pm. Snow. Sent to farm to repair rear tube in H.C's bike. Cleaned and tidied bench in tool shed. C. Wrycroft also on the pears 11am – 3 pm.
Wed.5.	Pruning pears all day.
Thur.6.	Pears until dinner. Painted last 7 rows. D. Foster came – went to look at trees behind Big Shed; topped one or two. Had breakfast in Big Shed as Charlie Preston repairing ladders there and had a fire going.
Fri.7.	Started pruning first row of damsons along road, with H.H. and F.R. Money 11.50 am. Took two saws to factory at dinner time and waited until 3.30pm to have them sharpened and a new handle fitted to one.
Sat.8.	One hour late owing to alarm clock! Damsons with H.H. and F.R.

W/E.Feb.15.1947

Mon.10.	Pruning Damsons with H.H. and F.R.
Tues.11.	Ditto. I lit a fire for breakfast.
Wed.12.	Ditto. F.R went to put in some Rivers trees. He lit a fire at 7 am, I made it up and put it right about 8.15 am.
Thur.13.	With H.H., F.R. and C. Newman: Mansfield headland – planting young Rivers and Yellows (where every other old Yellow was pulled up) until 12 o'clock, then back on the Damsons with H.H.
Fri.14.	H.H. did not turn up today. On the Damsons on my own all day.
Sat.15.	Damsons. H.H. not here. F.R. and C. Newman came 10 am to 1 pm to help.

W/E.Feb.22.1947

Mon.17.	Damsons with H.H. and F.R. C.N. and O. pulling out and burning. Took 2 saws for sharpening after dinner; back about 3 pm.
Tue.18.	Damsons with H.H.
Wed.19.	Ditto. Mr Chambers came and I went to Nursery Shed with him; got tar and brush etc. Heated the tar and

painted some pears. Took tar to Cawcutts mess hut before dinner. Made a hay-box after dinner; was just getting the tar warm (2pm) when H.C. sent me to the blacksmiths for draw-bar and frost studs. Back at 3.30pm.

Went to Cawcutts and painted trees.

Thur.20.　　Cawcutts – painting young trees in Laxtons. Heated the stuff in mess hut. Helped to fill muck; thawed out pipes in the tank house and lagged them with bags of straw. Did this between painting, while waiting for tar to heat up.

Fri.21.　　Repaired front tube of H.C's bike. Pruning Damsons with H.H., F.R. and C.W. Took saws to be sharpened after breakfast. Damsons until dinner. Snow. Cleared up in barn. Put mustard seed in dry bags, etc. Cleared up seeds in loft and cleared nest of mice. Saw an owl under the loft.

Sat.22.　　Stayed at home and got some wood from Travis & Arnold's: 5 x 10'6" of 1 ½ in x 2 in. Made a sawing horse and sawed up some wood with Geoff.

W/E.Mar.1.1947

Mon.24.　　Very cold in morning. Herbert and Fred did not come. I helped Tommy and Wally to pull out wood and burn until 3.15 pm. Then Mr Wrycroft came and we went on the Damsons; sun came out and a little warmer.

Tue.25.　　Sore throat and stayed at home.

NB. No further entries for the week – assumed off sick for remainder of week.

W/E.Mar.8.1947

Mon.3.　　Started Pruning Damsons opposite Big Shed, with H.H., K.F. and C.C. Had an hour for dinner today *Daylight hours 'pulling out' so we revert to leaving off at 5 pm].*

Took 2 sets long-arms to blacksmith's after breakfast. Called for long-arms after dinner and waited while small ones were repaired (new hook, blade and wire, and handle taken off the big ones). To call for the others tomorrow.

Tue.4.　　Damsons with H.H., K.F., and C.C. Went to blacksmith's after breakfast for the other long-arms – new hook, wire, blade and a new lever. C. Wrycroft there on my return. Sunny – F.R. able to spray after breakfast.

Wed.5.　　Damsons with H.H. and F.R. Snowed on and off all day. Car half off Stanley's road in snow drift; 3pm Mr Chambers told us about car; helped Fred to get tractor and pulled out car and took it to house. I drove the tractor back, changing gear etc.

	Difficult cycling to work this morning.
Thur.6.	Not at work owing to heavy fall of snow during the night.
Fri.7.	Damsons with H.H. Money about 12 noon.
Sat.8.	Damsons " " until 10.45 am. Started walking to Poultry Farm to get snow scrapers. Met Reg Pettit with two scrapers. Took one of them and walked down Starlings road; then helped him, B.Butler, Nobby, Tommy Sewell and Wally to clear snow from gateway down to Dumas House. Took 2 scrapers back to Poultry Farm and put in mixing shed.

W/E.Mar.15.1947

Mon.10.	Damsons with H.H., C.C., and K.F. Finished them up to the Rivers by 11 am. Started on first row opposite Big Shed (up side of young pears). C.C. and K.F. went back on gages after dinner. I stayed up farm and repaired puncture in front tube of Mr Chambers' bike. Cleared up tools in tool shed, then back on the damsons with Herbert until 5 pm.
Tue.11.	Ditto as Mon. with H.H. Finished row about 2.30 pm. K.F. came with us about 11.30 am (ready for spraying). C.W. came about 3 pm., H.C. came about 3.15 pm. Started on the 'goers' along water-course (same side as Big Shed).
Wed.12.	Ditto with H.H. (Ken spraying from about 10.30). Took our two saws as I went to dinner. Left them and went to farm Cleared up mess of grass seed in corner in loft; caught and killed 40 young mice. Went to fetch the sharpened saws. Back down the fen. Doug Foster had come on his motor bike while I was away - leaving as I got back. Pie (paid); Bought rabbit (1/6d – to be paid for).
Thur.13.	Ditto with H.H. and K.F. until 8 am. In Big Shed owing to rain until dinner time – cleaning and painting ladders. On damsons again (with H.H. only) until 5 pm. Ditch overflowing and flooding orchards; F.R, K.F. and W.B. cutting channels in afternoon to let water off. Should have been done in the morning (across bridge, and not at sides of ditch where they made them).
Fri.14.	Started on the Red Egg Plums at back of Nursery shed, with H.H. and K.F.
Sat.15.	Ditto with H.H. I lit a fire for breakfast at Big Shed.

Mon.17.   Red Eggs with H.H. until 12.30pm.   H.C. came and told me
               I am wanted on spraying. Helped to carry main across from
               opposite side to same side as Big Shed.
               Spraying damsons and Czars after dinner   (very heavy
               going).

Tue.18.   Spraying ditto until about 11 am.   Carried main, hose etc.
               onto road and helped load up Curly. Pruning Red Eggs with
               H.H. and C.W. and Pete Cook [?] after dinner. I felt rotten
               all day.

Wed.19.   Stayed abed until about 4.30 pm.
Thur.20.   "   "   "   "   12 noon.
Fri.21.   Rain. Went to Big Shed with H.H. and painted 3 pairs of
               steps.   Red Eggs after breakfast for the rest of the day.
               Money about 12 noon.

Sat.   Red Eggs with H.H.

W/E.Mar 29.1947

Mon.24.   Red Eggs until 2.20 pm.   Rain.   Big Shed – painted some
               more steps and a stool.   Cleared up in shed; used a bag on a
               fork as a brush.   Note: Curly brought 1 knapsack sprayer
               down at breakfast time. He brought spraying table about 11
               am, also sprays, drums, pails etc.

Tue.25.   Started pruning Red Eggs.   H.C. came and told us to get
               ready for spraying after breakfast.   Mixed up spray.
               Spraying all day in Mansfield (finished as far as the Baldwin
               blackcurrants).   Left tackle in barrel on its side.

Wed.26.   Red Eggs, owing to slight rain and apples being wet. Took
               spraying tackle into shed first thing.   Went to farm for
               staples for Long-arms; cleared up shed. Red Eggs.

Thur.27.   Finished spraying Mansfield 11.30 am., with H.H.   On Red
               Eggs after dinner.   Curly fetched the spraying tackle about
               3.30 pm and took it to Stanley's nursery.

Fri.28.   Sprayed the apples in Stanley's nursery and finished there
               about 9.20 am. Late breakfast in Big Shed.   Red Eggs after
               breakfast until 5 pm. Money about 11 am.

Sat.29.   Pruning Red Eggs. John picking up wood. Pearse and Peter
               were ploughing in the young pears.   Mr Chambers came 8
               am —I decided to have 2/6d per week stopped out of wages
               for National Savings.   H.C. told us to lift the bottom
               branches off the Yellow Egg plums at Park Farm next
               Monday when we have finished the Red Eggs.

_Mon.31. With H.H. Finished Red Eggs approx. 9.45 am. Mr Chambers told us about filling in gooseberries *[planting new bushes in gaps]*. We started to fill in the Whinhams.
Percy Bowers was ploughing.

Tues.1. H.H. We finished the Whinhams 8 am. Pearse ploughing. Packed up baskets near manure heap. We went to Park Farm:- H.H. started to saw off low branches on Gages and Yellows, so horses can get under to plough. I started to get up the gage suckers along fence (½ inch to 2 ½ inch diameter and numerous smaller ones). Sid Parker digging along one row (6 feet wide approx.). *[I think that Sid had now reached retiring age and had been kept on for helping out with general jobs].*

Wed.2. With H.H. sawing off branches until breakfast time. I did suckers after breakfast, which I finished about 11 am. We finished the trees by 2.30 pm. Started in Stanley's Orchard: We went first to Nursery Shed to get 2 ladders and my Long-arms, which we carried to S. Orchard, on our bikes. I left the twivel at the farm on the way.

Thur.3. Went to Stanley's Orchard. Mr Chambers came about 8 am and we went down the fen: filled in 3 trees on Mansfield (2 Worcesters and 1 ?). Took the rest of the young trees, also Whinham gooseberries, to Stanley's Nursery and put them in. Then back in Stanley's Orchard pruning.

Fri.4. Good Friday – Holiday.

Sat.5. Should have gone to work, but didn't.

Mon.7. Easter Monday – Holiday.

Tues.8. With H.H. pruning in Stanley's Orchard. After breakfast H.C. sent me to farm to repair puncture in rear tube of his bike, also adjusted chain and oiled bike. Cycled to Cambridge for Edgar to get two drinks from Runciman's (the Vet's) for Mare. Helped Edgar to feed foal, etc. Back in Orchard about 12.50 pm. H.C. asked me to go to the farm in the morning.

Wed.9. Farm. Cleared up the tool shed; took some tools up into loft. Got the old White Pony in from the yard round the back and gave her a curry down – still not clean! Took her out about 11 am with set of harrows and started to harrow grass in front of farm (other side of water) [?]

Thur.10.	Harrowing all day – same pony, same field.
Fri.11.	Finished field and went in the Vics. *[Victoria Plums]* alongside Cawcutts Road.
Sat.12.	Finished the Vic. Field at 1 o'clock. Got a load of wood in afternoon for myself (near Mansfield Road) *[presumably with permission, and the use of the pony and lorry].*
Sun.13.	Took bag of corn to Hammond's Field for Fred Reeder (tractor driver), and Charlie Preston (maintenance man) who were drilling oats. Broke gate lock key!

W/E.April 19.1947

Mon.14.	The old white Pony – Harrowing strawberries cross-ways on field 32. (Bill horse-hoeing it long ways).
Tues.15.	Boxer – harrowing oats in Hammond's field – got about half done; horse knocked up – not done much work lately.
Wed.16.	Old white Pony – harrowing as yesterday in Hammond's. Gave her 5 minutes rest at each end. Did not do quite half as much as yesterday.
Thur.17.	Boxer in Hammond's. Finished at dinner time, went round the headlands twice. On the gooseberries with strawberry harrow in the afternoon.
Fri.18.	Water carting for poultry etc. with Boxer:- 1st load: 3 tanks near mixing place and 1 tub in first headers. 2nd: 6 houses round plums. 3rd: German prisoners. 4th: field back of Woodhouse. 5th: load set down at dinner time – ditto as 4th after dinner. 6th: Finished Woodhouse field and orchard tub.
Sat.19.	Horse-hoeing in gooseberries with Boxer. Finished bottom field and started on top. (Only did middle rows between gooses and did not go up sides of trees as they are closer on top side). One round up each bay.

W/E.April 26.1947

Mon.21.	Horse-hoeing top gooseberries in pears, with Boxer. Finished about 4.20 pm.
Tues.22.	Water cart for poultry. Went for another load after dinner but was only able to get a little as the pump at Cawcutts had gone wrong. Load of mangolds to Park Farm; helped Travary *[German prisoner ?]* to unload his.
Wed.23.	1 load water to finish Piggots Field. 1 load mangolds after breakfast (Oswald's to Woodhouse. 1 load mangolds to Impington Farm – tipped up. Rain. After dinner threw out

	muck from corner box to Percy and Ernie. Mangold cleaning; chaff, etc.
Thur.24.	Horse-hoeing gooses in front of Nursery Shed, with Boxer. Did about ¾ of the bit, and should finish about 11.30 tomorrow.
Fri.25.	Finished gooses about 10.30 am; horse-hoeing Mansfield for the rest of the day.
Sat.26.	Water cart for poultry. 1st load from Park to Woodhouse. Breakfast. 2nd load Woodhouse; 3rd load – Germans, poultry and fen.

W/E.May 3.1947

Mon.28.	Water cart for the Sprayers (Cawcutts Road) with Boxer. First load from Park Farm.
Tue.29.	Ditto yesterday – Cawcutts Road, Plots etc. until 12 noon. 1 load in afternoon to Nursery Shed (for Mansfield).
Wed.30.	Water cart for poultry – 3 loads. Threw load of mangolds through shed window, and cleaned same. Harrowing in afternoon on Mansfield with Boxer. David Peck also, using Edgar's horse-hoe. Ernie Cross's last day.
Thur.1.	Horse-hoeing on Mansfield; David Peck also. RAIN. Back to farm after breakfast. 1 load mangolds, Oswald's Road to Farm shed. 1 Load mangolds, Oswald's Road to Farm (set down), David ditto. Dinner. Afternoon: I unloaded both loads and then got 2 more, and David 1 more. I emptied one and tipped the last one.
Fri.2.	Water Cart for the Sprayers with Boxer. (Pears down the fen) 3 loads in morning. Afternoon: one load to Germans, one load to sprayers. Very cold, with strong North wind and rain on and off. Felt a cold coming on!
Sat.3.	Stayed at home.

W/E.May 10.1947

No Entries – presumably off sick/

W/E.May17.1947

Mon.12.	Mr Chambers ill – Mr Wrycroft acting foreman. In the drill shed, helping Edgar to change blades for points on spring-tine cultivator. No proper points; picked up a bundle of points with my bike, from between apples and blackberries. Wrong ones! But made do. Leading for Edgar in blackcurrants on Mansfield. Blacksmith came after dinner to do Mare's foot.

Tue.13.	Leading for Edgar in blackcurrants until dinner. Driving for Bill after dinner, with three horses – Tom, Punch and Short. First time I have driven 2 trace horses. (Ground very hard where the tractor and sprayer had been).
Wed.14.	Ditto yesterday with Bill. Went round the strawberry headland on way to dinner and back, and on the way home at 4.30 pm. *[This would have been with the cultivator].*
Thur.15.	Ditto yesterday. Finished in the young gooseberries about 2 pm. And started on the Nursery bit. Very hard – went round the strawberry headland and the cabbage headland on way to dinner and back.
Fri.16.	Ditto as yesterday.
Sat.17.	Warm. Potato carting from station to the poultry farm (3 loads). One load of chaff and dust etc. from the Rickyard to Cawcutts Plots, to burn.

W/E.May 24.1947

Mon.19.	Small water cart of water to poultry houses round the plums. One load to Big Shed for the sprayers – had to wait to see if they required it. One load to poultry. One load to Germans, ducks etc. Two loads to chick field and the back of Stanley's for Piggott.
Tue.20.	2 good loads mangolds and one smaller load to Park Farm. After dinner took Tom to the Blacksmith's, but he was not there. Another load of mangolds to Park Farm. Was a few minutes late in stable.
Wed.21.	Took Tom in cart to the blacksmith's to be shod. Brought repaired horse-hoe wheel home. Took ¾ load of mangolds to Park Farm – which finished off the pit. Loaded cart with rotten mangolds and set it down at the Farm. Unloaded it after dinner, at Cawcutts muck-heap, then got another load, which cleared them up.
Thur.22.	Water-cart for the sprayers all day. Warm. 1½ hours overtime.
Fri.23.	Warm. To Blacksmith's with Boxer; then took him to Edgar. Took Edgar's horse to Blacksmith; took Rufus to Blacksmith's; took Punch to Blacksmith's. (Took Edgar's horse to him on my return; took Tom from him to Percy and took Rufus from Percy. No time for dinner – 1½ hours overtime.
Sat.24.	*To London on 1 o'clock train from Cambridge to stay with the family of my friend Derek Maish.*

W/E.May 31.1947

Mon.26./Tues.27.   Staying at Derek's.

Wed.28.   Back at work. Tidying up garage and tool shed etc. Helped Curly with one load of silverleaf and collected tools from Big Shed and Nursery Shed with him.

Thur.29.   Horse-hoeing strawberries on field 41 with Tom, where David had left off. Hot.

Fri.30.   Ditto – finished strawberries about 11.15 am. Hot. Went to farm: swept stable, then helped to carry in rations. Potato carting – two loads from Poultry Farm to Cawcutts. (What's the idea?!)

Sat.31.   Water-cart for sprayers – 5 loads. Also filled up Bull tanks. Hot.

W/E.June7.1947

Mon.2.   Water-cart for poultry with Tom in small water cart. Hot. One load to little chickens at back of farm; back to Cawcutts to fill up. Breakfast at Cawcutts. Another load to Stanley's. Third load to finish Stanley's and in Stanley's orchard. Filled cart again and set it down in farm, for dinner. Two loads down the fen after dinner; Nobby had a pail full for tractor. <u>NB</u>.: Some Strawberries Ripe.

Tue.3.   Swath-turning on the Forty-Acre with Tom in side-delivery rake. David Peck doing the same. We worked until 8 pm; no tea; 3 hours overtime. <u>NB</u>.: Took the rake from the Farm in the morning; had to hook up the backing chains tight, so that Tom would noy catch his back feet on the front wheel while transporting it. Took off the britching on the field. Sweat!!

Wed.4.   Rowing up hay with Tom in side-delivery rake – 4 swaths to a row. David Peck ditto. Warm and very breezy – wind a nuisance when working against it. Poles sent to heap up from about 10 am., Jack Campbell, Ted Newman and C. Wrycroft also heaping up after tea. Finished rowing up at about 7.20 pm.

Thur.5.   To Park Farm; collected Tom and took him to Blacksmith to have new offside back shoe put on. Back about 9.15 am and had breakfast at Park Farm. Four Cats. Repaired puncture in each wheel of Mr Chambers' bike; got a new tyre at J. Bull's and fitted that. Greased the Strawberry Dry Sprayer. Dinner. Went to the factory with Boxer and collected the iron-wheeled lorry that had been repaired. Took load of fan

	rubbers [?] down Oswald's Road for Charlie Preston. Put on floor of shed. Cool.
Fri.6.	Helped Curly get chip baskets and weighing machines to strawberry field ready for the start of the strawberry picking. First day's picking with me recording the weights for the pickers.
Sat.7.	Picking / weighing / recording strawberries.

W/E.June14.1947

Mon.9. to Fri.13. Strawberries each day.

Sat.14.   *Start of my week's cycling holiday with my friend Frank Dixon, staying mainly at Youth Hostels. Left Cambridge 8 am today and cycled to King's Lynn – 45 miles.*

W/E.June 21.1947

Mon.16.	*King's Lynn to Sheringham – 41 miles*
Tues.17.	*Stayed in Sheringham*
Wed.18.	*Sheringham to Norwich, via Yarmouth - 53 miles*
Thur.19.	*Norwich to Croxton, via Attleborough and Thetford – 30 miles.*
Fri.20.	*Stayed at Croxton*
Sat.21.	*Croxton to King's Lynn, via East Dereham and Swaffham – 47 miles*
Sun.22.	*King's Lynn to Cambridge – 45 miles.*

Note: During the nights at Sherringham, Norwich and Croxton we would have stayed at Youth Hostels. On the two 'King's Lynn' nights we stayed at my Dad's Uncle 'Dick' Marsters and Aunt Mabel, at North Wootton, just outside Lynn.

W/E.June 28 and W/E.July 5.   Booking Strawberries the whole of both weeks.

W/E.July12.1947

Mon.7.	Booking Strawberries – field 50.
Tue.8.	Booking Whinham Gooseberries – field 32A; finished 1 pm.
	Booking Strawberries – field 50 after dinner. Rain 4 pm.
Wed.9.	Ditto – field 50.
Thur.10.	" " "
Fri.11.	" " " (finished 10.30 am).
	Tying up trees (Victorias) in orchard next to Cawcutts Road – Bill Butler and pickers Nos. 6, 7, 8, 9, 28 and 77.

Sat.12.	Tying up Czars down the fen. With Nos. 28, 77 and Bill Butler.

W/E.July19.1947

Mon.14.	With Bill and the women; sorting potatoes in Cawcutts rick-yard until 10 am; cutting 20 bags cabbages until 11.30 am. Tying up Czars for the rest of the day.
Tue.15.	Tying up Czars all day; (cabbages tomorrow).
Wed.16.	Cabbages until dinner time. After dinner, picking up potatoes, where Edgar had opened up the stitches ready for the tractor to spin them out..
Thur.17.	Cabbages until 3.45 pm, then on the Czars.
Fri.18.	Tying up Czars all day.
Sat.19.	Picking up spuds and loading onto Whitehead lorries. Rain about 11.30 am.

W/E.July 26.1947

Mon.21.	Cutting cabbages, tying up bags and loading until 3.30pm. (to Farm about 12.30pm to mend puncture, and had to get a spring-link for the chain, on Mr Chambers' bike) Helped unload LMS lorry of fruit boxes at corner of Red Eggs, field 33.
Tue.22.	Picked Rivers Plums – Mansfield (finished 11 am). Started on Rivers, field 31B. Picking over the ripest; called out at 4 pm. Went to farm to do the books. Back to fen; helped to chip the plums that were in boxes. Helped load up Whitehead lorry with 380 x 12 lb. chips (including 102 from Mansfield).
Wed.23.	Rivers – 31B and 31A (picking over). 664 x 12 lb chips, 500 of which Whitehead took about 5.15 pm. Curly took some ladders to Stanley's Orchard ready for morning
Thur.24.	Rivers in Stanley's Orchard – (stripping).
Fri.25.	Finished in Stanley's 10 am., Did 31A by 1 pm – stripping. One third of the way up 31B in afternoon. Loading Whitehead (500) 5.30 pm.
Sat.26.	Cutting Cabbages and tying bags (180 bags).

W/E.Aug.2.1947 – Booking Fruit all week

NB: Diary entries were omitted from this point for the remainder of the fruit picking period and then recommenced in October 1947

W/E.Oct.18.1947 Mon.13 – Sat.18. With horses – Corn carting all week.

W/E.Oct.25.1947

Mon.20.	)
Tue.21.	) Corn and Bag Manure carting.
Wed.22.	)

Thur.23.   Getting suckers off gooseberries, 7 am – 5 pm. Top side of Field 31 – Careless. Using 'spud' to get those in the ground; pulling off the ones on the bush. John Welch with me from 8 am.

Fri.24.   Ditto as yesterday; Douglas picking up pieces until about 11 am, when he was sent on watering cabbages.

Sat.25.   Gooseberry suckers.

W/E.Nov.1.1947

Mon.27.   Gooseberry suckers; Douglas picking up; 7 am – 4 pm. Mr Chambers came and told us to look in 'Big' and 'Nursery' sheds for any tools left there. Glad of a little shelter as wind very strong and cold.

Tue.28.   Farm: sorting and making list of tools in the loft. Corn bags from under the big cart lodge to the loft. Breakfast. After breakfast went round with Charlie Wrycroft, looking for and asking about tools. Apple Shed: helped F.R. weigh up some Laxtons and Newtons and load up Whitehead lorry. Back on Gooses 4 – 5 pm.

Wed.29.   Gooseberries, alone all day. Tommy and Jack hoeing each day and they made fires in Nursery Shed for breakfast. It looked like rain first thing, but didn't get any.

Thur.30.   Gooseberry suckers until 12 noon. C. Wrycroft and Doug. Foster came: told me to stop suckering for now, as they would want some cuttings and it was too early yet to get them.

Fri.31.   Pruning Blackcurrants all day with Charlie Camps. T. Sewell and J. Campbell hoeing in the blackcurrants. Warmer than yesterday, but gradually got colder and breezy.

Sat.1.   Ditto Blackcurrants / ditto hoeing, as yesterday. Cold first thing, warmer later.

W/E.Nov.8.1947

Mon.3.   Pruning Blackcurrants with Charlie. Slight thunderstorm about 4 pm for about twenty minutes; enough to make the ground 'pick up'. Sunny before, but cold after.

Tue.4.	Ditto Blackcurrants. Slight drizzle 4 – 4.30 pm; ground still damp on top and picking up a bit. Tommy and Jack sowing potash – about 1 bag to 2 bays.
Wed.5.	Currants all day.
Thur.6.	Pruning currants 7 – 8 am. Un-tying trees until dinner time (left too long, strings now cutting into the trunks). Pruning currants after dinner.
Fri.7.	H.C. sent me to pick up 2 hoes and 2 overcoats of the Poles, and take to Park Farm. (Poles not sent because of Poultry Disease). NB: Find out about Pole's rations (double ours ?)
Sat.8.	Currants with C.C. until breakfast. H.C. told me to feed the poultry in the peaches and the meadow, also sheep and dog [?]. Back on the Blackcurrants about 12 noon and we finished the last row of the Westwicks by 1 o'clock.

W/E.Nov.15.1947

Mon.10.	Fed sheep and dog. Watered and disinfected straw on Stanley's Road and in gateway at back of farm. Sent to gravel pit to tell Claud to start carting potatoes off rail. Pruning apples on Mansfield with Charlie Camps.
Tues.11.	Fed sheep and dog and watered hens in peaches. Ditto for straw and apples as yesterday.
Wed.12.	Disinfected roads after breakfast. Apple pruning. NB: Gets too dark to see to prune properly by 4.45 pm. Will probably start half-hour dinner time shortly.
Thur.13.	Apples all day with C.C. Doug Foster came about 10 – 11.30 am. He said that we are doing OK. Except that I am leaving the top leads slightly too long. Douglas (not Foster) picking up apple wood after dinner.
Fri.14.	Apples all day with C.C. Douglas picking up after dinner.
Sat.15.	Apples with C.C.
	Went to Herbert Webb's at Coton in afternoon: pruned his espalier apple, also a standard tree. Had a go with his Trusty Tractor and plough. Very cold wind.

W/E.Nov.22.1947

Mon.17.	Pruning Mansfield Apples with C.C. all day. NB: started different working times today – 7.30 am – 4.30 pm (½ hours dinner at 12 noon).
Tues.18.	Ditto apples with C.C. I had a go with Walter Coxall's plough today. Cold & Frosty.
Wed.19.	Ditto " " " Weather ditto.
Thur.20.	Ditto. " " " Weather milder; slight rain at times.

| Fri.21. | Finished apples and started in the Mendip blackcurrants. |
| Sat.22. | No entry. |

W/E.Nov.29.1947

Mon.24.	Leading horses for Walter in the gooseberries – ploughing.
Tues.25.	Ditto until about 8.30 am, then back on currants with C.C.
Wed.26.	Currants until 10.30 am. Doug Foster came with 14 young trees, which we planted in Stanley's Nursery. Dinner about 1 pm, then pruning currants.
Thur.27.	Currants with C.C.
Fri.28.	Finished currants. Finished apples in corner near Nursery Shed by dinner time. Pruning in the Pears, opposite shed, after dinner.
Sat.29.	Pears with C.C.

W/E.Dec.6.1947

Mon.1.	Pruning Pears with C.C. Bill Butler and women pruning Gooseberries. Frosty.
Tue.2.	Ditto Pears. Frosty. Got to work early and got bag of roots for breakfast fire. NB: the Conference pear wood is not so tough to cut as other. .
Wed.3.	Ditto Pears. Not so cold; rain from about 3 pm.
Thur.4.	Ditto Pears. Slight drizzle all day; mud picking up a lot.
Fri.5.	Started on top side of Young Pears (top side) about 11 am. Wind; rain on and off.
Sat.6.	Pruning Young Pears. Weather fine.

W/E.Dec.13.1947

Mon.8.	Pruning Young Pears with C.C. Mild, but rain on and off.
Tue.9.	Ditto Pears.
Wed.10.	" "
Thur.11.	" " Started bottom side of road about 3 pm.
Fri.12.	Pruning Pears – bottom side.
Sat.13.	Ditto Pears until about 10.30 am when H.C. sent us to Stanley's Nursery to stake the 14 young trees that we had planted there.

W/E.Dec.20.1947

| Mon.15. | Pruning Young Pears. Helped Reg. And Pole to move the 'Monkey Winch' before and after dinner. [This is a hand operated winch for pulling out trees from the ground] |
| Tue.16. | Pruning Young Pears. Dull and wet. Had last injection this evening [?]. |

Wed.17.	Finished the Pears about 11 am. To Poultry Farm and started pruning the grafted trees in the pens. Had dinner in the Poles' place. Felt rotten all day. Bed after tea.
Thur.18.	Stayed abed until about 2 pm.
Fri.19.	Pruning the grafted Apple trees in the laying-shed pen.
Sat.20.	Showed a new chap the way to Bill Butler who was in the young blackberries. Tidied up the loft (had to move steps and get in through window, as the keys have been lost. Tidied up in the Barn; swept the stable; mended puncture in H.C's bike. Cleaned and ground up 4 bushels mangolds and then cleaned some more.

W/E.Dec.27.1947

Mon.22.	Pruning the Grafted Apples on the Poultry Farm.
Tue.23.	Ditto yesterday.
Wed.24-Sun.28.	Off for Christmas.

W/E.Jan.3.1948

Mon.29.	Pruning Apples on the Poultry Farm. Started on Apples in the Geese-Field 10am.
Tue.30.	Took pruning saws to th factory to be sharpened 8 am; took pick to Blacksmith's and waited while it was sharpened; called for the saws on the way back to the farm. Sawing off dead branches in the pens before dinner, then pruning Apples.
Wed.31.	Pruning Apples on the Poultry Farm.
Thur.1.	Ditto Apples. Biked to Nursery Shed at 8 am to fetch the 'spud' for getting up suckers. H.C. sent me to count the trays in the Potato shed. Dinner 15 minutes late. Finished getting up suckers 1.20 pm, then back on Pruning. Charlie broke the spring in his secateurs.
Fri.2.	Finsihed pruning the Apples at the Poultry Farm about 9.30 am. Sent down to Mansfield to count Missing Blackcurrants:-

	Mendips	52
	Westwicks	225
	Baldwins	142
	Hattons	30

Finished about 4.15 pm. Weather very mild; rain from about 3 pm.

| Sat.3. | Counting Missing Gooseberries with Charlie Camps and Fred Reeder – finished about 11 am. Started pruning Damsons and Red Eggs Plums; taking out broken, dead and crossing wood on the Damsons; taking out young shoots |

going out of the tops of the Red Eggs, plus crossing and crowded wood, and topping some of the young wood low down on the trees. Weather: Muggy.

<u>W/E.Jan.10.1948</u>

Mon.5.	Pruning Red Eggs and Damsons on Field 33.
Tue.6.	Ditto yesterday, with C. Camps and Bill, a new chap. Me on the long-arm pruners.
Wed.7.	Ditto yesterday. Mild, rain on and off all afternoon.
Thur.8.&Fri.9.	" "
Sat.10.	Finished the Damsons and Red Eggs about 9 am and started on the Gages at corner.
	Doug Foster came in van about 10 am and took C.C. and me to Stanley's Nursery to plant more trees. Then back on the Greengages until 1 o'clock.

-------------ooOoo------------

146